Walking the Path

A handbook for spiritual practice

General Church of the New Jerusalem
Bryn Athyn, Pennsylvania
2021

ISBN 9780945003816

Library of Congress Control Number: 2021917421

Table of Contents

In this book I have used the customary abbreviations for Swedenborg's Writings. Here is a key to those abbreviations:

AC	*Arcana Coelestia*
AE	*Apocalypse Explained*
AR	*Apocalypse Revealed*
Char	*Doctrine of Charity* (in *Posthumous Theological Works*)
DLW	*Divine Love and Wisdom*
DP	*Divine Providence*
EU	*Earths in the Universe*
Faith	*Doctrine of Faith*
HD	*The New Jerusalem and Its Heavenly Doctrine*, also called *Heavenly Doctrine*
HH	*Heaven and Hell*
ISB	*Interaction Between the Soul and Body*
Life	*Doctrine of Life*
LJ	*Last Judgment*
LJP	*Last Judgment, Posthumous*
Lord	*Doctrine of the Lord*
ML	*Married Love*, also called *Conjugial Love*
SE	*Spiritual Experiences*, also known as *Spiritual Diary*
SS	*Doctrine of the Sacred Scripture*
TCR	*True Christian Religion*
Verbo	*De Verbo* (in *Posthumous Theological Works*), also called *The Word of the Lord from Experience*

About this book

In this book I offer a picture of the eight main activities we can engage in to grow as spiritual beings and to live a life of service. These eight activities change us. They build the habits and practices that most fully allow us to act with love and integrity.

Being a good person means following the Lord. If we obey the Ten Commandments and the Golden Rule because it's what the Lord says, we'll do well in life. Yet when we try to be good, loving people, we discover that a little knowledge is often not enough. In the areas we care about, we invest time and energy in a deeper understanding of how to accomplish our goals. This book offers a deeper view of what living a compassionate, thoughtful life looks like.

My approach

This book is a companion to a longer book, *Exploring the Path: An in-depth guide to the spiritual practices involved in becoming a loving person*. The book you are holding presents the main ideas and actions from the longer book without many of the deeper doctrinal explanations. At times I have put "See *Exploring the Path*" with a page reference for those who want to dig into the more developed ideas in the longer book.

I believe that all of Swedenborg's Writings have Divine authority. They are the Word on the same level as Scripture, words of infinite love and wisdom. Throughout this book I say "the Lord says" when quoting both Scripture and Swedenborg's Writings. I recognize that not everyone gives that same level of authority to these texts, and I invite you to consider them at your own level of belief and conviction.

A word about translation: Where the original language will support it, I have changed gendered pronouns, most often by changing the text to say "we" rather than "he." I have also sometimes deliberately used feminine pronouns, even in quotations, to remind us that most of the time both men and women are meant when the third person singular pronoun is used. That said, I have occasionally used "he" and "him" to refer to all people where changing it would obscure the meaning.

Acknowledgments

Writing about our spiritual lives is like trying to take a picture of the universe. It is far too big a topic to wrap our minds around, and any one person's perspective is limited. So I am deeply grateful to the people who have read through drafts of the book and made suggestions. Chuck Ebert, Tania Alden, Rev. Robert Junge, and Rev. Ethan McCardell read parts of the book and gave me valuable feedback. Rev. Jared Buss, Rt. Rev. Peter Buss Sr., Bronwen Henry, and my wife Ann read the whole book and offered detailed suggestions. Ann read it multiple times. Donna

Carswell served as the final proofreader. It is much better because of their input and even more so because of their care for the project. Insight in spiritual matters comes when we put our hearts and lives into a subject, and I know I have benefitted from the wisdom and insight of my readers. And finally, although I did most of the research and writing of this book on my own time, my boss Rev. Eric Carswell encouraged me to use work time to finish up the project, for which I am deeply grateful.

I am so grateful that I am able to spend my days exploring what the Lord teaches and sharing it with others and that I am part of an organization that is dedicated to creating a culture based on what He says. I hope this book helps to develop the dialog about how we can love one another and the Lord better by building practices of love and charity into our lives.

Come, and let us go up to the mountain of Jehovah, to the house of the God of Jacob. And He will teach us of His ways, and we shall walk in His paths. For out of Zion shall go forth the law, and the word of Jehovah from Jerusalem. (Is 2:3)

A new commandment I give to you, that you love one another; as I have loved you, that you also love one another. By this all will know that you are My disciples, if you have love for one another. (John 13:34-35)

"But what do you think? A man had two sons, and he came to the first and said, 'Son, go, work today in my vineyard.' He answered and said, 'I will not,' but afterward he regretted it and went. Then he came to the second and said likewise. And he answered and said, 'I go, sir,' but he did not go. Which of the two did the will of his father?" (Matt 21:28-31)

Charity Is the Focus
of Spiritual Living

*The whole of Sacred Scripture is nothing else than teachings about love
and charity. (AC 6632)*

Many of us have tried to be loving, kind, useful people and have come face to face
with our own failings. Spiritual work is hard, and sometimes even a lifetime can
seem too short for us to become the people we want to be.

At the same time, spiritual work is rewarding. We work to love others, and we
see a change. We find blessings beyond the effort we put in—peace and joy that are
gifts from the Lord, connections with others that offer safety and support, a sense
of meaning and direction in our lives.

Part of the reason becoming kind and loving people is hard is that love, by itself,
is not enough. We need tools and practices to support us on our journey of becoming loving people. This book offers some of those tools and practices. By "practices"
I mean any activity, whether within ourselves or visible to others, that we consciously choose to engage in to become better people.

WE EXIST TO LOVE

We know, almost without being told, that we are in this world to learn to love the
Lord and others. The Lord teaches this powerfully:

> The first of all the commandments is: "Hear O Israel, the Lord our God, the Lord is
> One. And you shall love the Lord your God with all your heart, with all your mind,
> with all your soul, and with all your strength." This is the first commandment. And
> the second, like it, is this: "You shall love your neighbor as yourself." There is no
> other commandment greater than these. (Mark 12:29-31)

> The one great truth [of spiritual life] is that love to the Lord and love for the neigh-
> bor are first and foremost. (AC 4776)

Everything we do or think about is designed by the Lord to lead to our learning
to love. It is a common teaching that "there is only one doctrine, namely, that of
love to the Lord and of charity toward the neighbor" (AC 3451:4). The Lord is very
clear that teaching, or doctrine, is really about how to love people.

When we love others, we serve them; we seek to act in a way that benefits them
(AE 707), as the Lord shows and teaches:

1

You call me Teacher and Lord, and you say well, for so I am. If I then, your Lord
and Teacher, have washed your feet, you also ought to wash one another's feet.
For I have given you an example, that you should do as I have done to you.
(John 13:13-15)

To love the Lord and the neighbor means in general to perform useful services.
(HH 112)

We are in this world to learn to love. Our journey here involves figuring out how
to love and choosing the path of love.

LOVE NEEDS TRUTH

Even though love is at the core of our lives, it cannot be achieved without its mate.
All desires are powerful but blind; that is why they need a mate. So the Lord gave
us that mate—the truth—that shows us how to love, as He teaches here:

If you love Me, keep My commandments. (John 14:15)

Every Divine truth is related to the following two commandments: Love God above
all things, and love your neighbor as yourself. These two commandments are the
base from which truths are derived, the reason why truths exist, and the end to
which truths lead—immediately or remotely. (AC 4353:3)

When we think about a truth by itself, it can seem like a cold, hard rule. But that
is not the truth about truth. Only when we see the love within a truth do we understand that truth. Our calling as a church and as human beings, then, is to learn the
truth so that we can know how to reject unloving behaviors and embrace loving
ones. Although this book is about charity, it consists almost entirely of truths that
teach us how to act from charity or goodwill (AC 8516:2). Truth is true because it
shows us how to act from love. Truth is the eyes of love.

LOVE AND TRUTH REALLY ARE INSEPARABLE

*Faith without love is not faith, and love without faith is not love. Love
receives its specific quality from faith and faith its life from love. (AC
9050:6; AC 9514)*

In daily life, it often seems that goodness or truth has to take the lead, that one of
them has to win out. People regularly ask variations of the same question: Is it better to be right and truthful or kind and merciful? Do I say or do what I believe is
right and risk alienating others? Do I say that your comment annoyed me, or do
I smile and pass it over? Do I forgive your unkind actions, or do I stand for what
is just and tell you how damaging it was?

We can try to be right without being kind or kind without being right. But then we end up where we don't want to be: Kindness without understanding is actually not kindness; and being right without kindness undermines the truth we see. We need to find a way to stand for truth while embracing love, to forgive while protecting our boundaries, to speak the truth while taking other people's feelings and needs into consideration. Goodness and truth are inseparable.

We go through times in which truth seems to predominate, and we compel ourselves to do what we know to be loving, overruling a lower part of ourselves that does not want to. A deep part of us wants to do what is right, to act from love, and we force ourselves to do this. Self-compulsion is as much an act of love as a spontaneous kind gesture, perhaps more so. Because it doesn't feel as good, we can discount it. "I forced myself to be nice, so I'm not really very loving," we might say. In time, we come to do what is right and kind with less effort, and that is precisely because we come to see that truth is simply the way we express love. The Lord has given us spiritual practices to help us on that journey of learning to spontaneously act from love, guided by truth.

SPIRITUAL PRACTICES

This book offers eight spiritual practices, practices that are love in action. They are the primary activities we should be engaging in, activities that open our hearts, minds, and lives to the Lord's inflowing life. There are three core, internal spiritual practices which lead us to heaven, and there are five external practices that support these three. In general, when I use the term "spiritual practice," I mean all eight activities. Sometimes I use it in the more conventional sense of describing the five external activities we can engage in.

Each of these practices leads us to be able to love the Lord and others better. As you read the Word, I invite you to ask, "How will this teaching enable me to be a more loving person?" As a very general rule, I would say that doing the internal practices will help us become more loving of our neighbors, and doing the external practices as well will enable us to elevate our kind deeds to make them acts of love, not just to our neighbors, but also to the Lord.

Eight Spiritual Practices

The life of charity is to practice goodness, sincerity, and justice from religion, thus because it is commanded by the Lord in the Word. (SE 5958)

We've been looking at what love or charity is. Now we'll look at patterns or practices we use to develop charity in our lives, which happens in two different ways. The first way is by an inner path: working on the deeper feelings and actions that make us heavenly people. The second is by an outer path: developing patterns or habits of living that support being a good person.

THE THREE CORE PRACTICES OF CHARITY

The three core practices of charity are 1) looking to the Lord, 2) shunning evil loves and deeds, and 3) doing what is good. Here are two teachings among many:

> The first element of charity is to look to the Lord and shun evils because they are sins, and the second element of charity is to do good deeds. (Char 40)

> People who look to the Lord and shun evils as sins, if they sincerely, justly, and faithfully do the work of their office and employment, become a form of charity. (Char 158; TCR 422)

The three core practices follow each other in order. First, turning to the Lord brings Him present, and His presence becomes the motivation for all that is spiritual in us. Then, when He is present in us, we are moved to shun evils because those evil actions and feelings would push Him away and hurt others. And finally, when we have done these first two, we express love by serving others (doing what is good).

Because New Church teaching is so clear about the importance and value of these three core practices, I am simply presenting them here. However, the value in the external or support spiritual practices is harder to see, so we will spend more time in this chapter exploring why they are important.

THE FIVE SUPPORT PRACTICES OF CHARITY

*Each of us acquires a disposition or nature from frequent practice or
habit, and that practice or habit from the things we have learned.
(AC 3843:2)*

This brings us to the external behaviors that support and give expression to our
deeper spiritual practices. Spiritual living is hard to measure; sometimes we can't
tell if we are being good people. So the Lord has given us foundational signs or
indicators of whether charity is present in us. Doctors look for the signs of a disease
so they can make a diagnosis; we look for signs that our friends are being honest
or are sad because we cannot actually see their inner intentions or feelings.

It may come as a surprise that the signs of love and charity in our lives are that
we're involved in what we'd think of as rituals: attending worship, reading the
Word, prayer, and the like. We may think of worship as a formality that has little
to do with the core of spiritual living; it is certainly unpopular and stigmatized in
today's secular culture. But worship is more than a formality.

Inner love always manifests itself in loving expressions. This is why the Lord
teaches us that "there is no internal quality without its sign and its indication" (Char
183). Worship, we're told, is that loving expression of a spiritual life, a way we and
others can see the inner qualities we are striving for. By way of analogy, imagine
a parent taking care of their child, dutifully doing all the things that parents do for
children, yet without showing the child any overt signs of love or affection. The acts
of care are the most important, just as living a good life is. But expressions of love
are also necessary signs if a parent is going to be effective. And the Lord tells us that
the signs of charity in us have to do with worship (DLW 431; Char 173-75, 177).

One passage describes the external elements of charity as attending church,
participating in Holy Supper, and the like, and internal charity as the qualities we've
spoken of above. It continues:

> With every member of the Church *both aspects must be present, the external and
> the internal. Unless both are present spiritual life does not exist with the person;*
> for the internal is so to speak the soul, and the external so to speak the body hous-
> ing the soul.... A concern for both exists with all who lead a good life in accor-
> dance with the teachings of their Church. (AC 8762:2).[1]

While we need to shun evil and do good, we also need to practice these external
signs. Another passage, after describing that living a good life is internal worship,
continues, "While a person is in the world, however, he or she ought certainly to

---

[1]Unless otherwise noted, all emphasis in quotations has been added by the author.

participate in external worship as well. For it is by external worship that internal things are aroused, and by means of external worship external things are kept holy so as to enable internal ones to flow in." (AC 1618). These teachings show us that good people need to be involved in an active life of worship, and there are many other passages that say the same thing (e.g., AC 7038, 8252; HH 222; AE 1061:3; see also AC 1175:2).

We may resist the idea that external practices matter. Modern culture quite rightly holds that our intentions and our deeper efforts are what count, especially in our spiritual lives. Because of this, it can be especially hard to engage in external spiritual practices that sometimes feel like going through the motions. But this does not mean that those external practices are unimportant. Our daily lives are full of useful rituals, from the rituals that sports players use to help them concentrate to the rituals we use to celebrate important holidays. External spiritual practices matter because they provide an opportunity for us to open ourselves up to the Lord's gifts.

The Lord invites us to create the foundation of a beautiful spiritual home by establishing strong spiritual practices. We have been put in this world to grow, to take on responsibility for our lives over time. Our pathway involves incorporating these spiritual practices into our lives, one by one.

If external practices or rituals are important, we could then ask which ones we should focus on. The Lord in the Word describes a number of things that good people do as external spiritual practices. These five are mentioned far more than any others:

- Attending church
- Taking Holy Supper
- Saying prayers
- Reading the Word and other spiritual books
- Thinking about spiritual matters and reflecting on one's life[1]

This is a list of transformative things we could work into our lives. These actions may not be new ideas to us, but how they can support us may be surprising.

THE BENEFITS OF THESE SPIRITUAL PRACTICES

The Lord lists many benefits of becoming involved in various external forms of worship (a term which includes practices like prayer, as well as attending church).

---

[1] For a more detailed explanation of why these five are the ones we should concentrate on, see *Exploring the Path*, 15-32.

We want to know what the benefit will be before we take up the challenge of developing new habits.

Spiritual Practices Call to Mind Deeper Spiritual Qualities

One benefit of these practices is that they bring our minds back to spiritual reality, to what will still be true in a thousand years. Daily life involves dealing with the people and situations in front of us. We may occasionally think about spiritual principles as they apply to the situation we are dealing with, and we may say a quick prayer in some circumstances, but most of daily living involves trying to be useful in the here and now. This is good and appropriate.

By contrast, in worship we are called to put aside those everyday concerns and to focus on something deeper: "To the extent people are removed from bodily and worldly interests their ideas are spiritual, that is, they are lifted up toward heaven, as happens when they are engaged in any kind of sacred worship" (AC 2411:2). One gift of worship is that we can, for a time, put away daily concerns to think about and experience deeper realities. Worship, in its various forms, is the means the Lord uses to lead us toward internal ways of living while we do our daily activities (AC 1083:1, 4).

Humility in Worship Brings the Lord's Presence

A major way in which we bring ourselves into that deeper state is by turning to the Lord with humility. Not only does humility open us to the Lord, but it also causes evil to go away: "Humility exists in those who worship the Lord and give Him glory. From those in whom humility exists the proprium or what belongs to self departs. So far as this departs, the Divine is received" (AC 10646:3).

Consider the ways in which worship develops humility:

- We encourage humility by our actions when we kneel to pray or bow our heads to receive a blessing.
- We show it by stopping in our busy lives to give time to the Lord.
- We build it when we limit our personal desires and ask how the Lord would like us to express ourselves.
- We create it by building the routines of our lives around the Lord's teaching.
- We support it by asking the Lord for help in prayer, by exploring the Lord's truth as we read His Word, and by receiving the bread and wine in the Holy Supper as a symbol of our need for His help.

The Lord's Presence Transforms Us

Whenever we invite the Lord into our lives, His presence affects and transforms us, often in ways that we may not notice. Think about how quickly your affection can change when you sit down in your favorite chair to relax while listening to your favorite music, or how a sudden feeling of compassion for someone you love can change your mental state and outlook in an instant. The Lord's presence creates a far more powerful change of state than these examples, and all spiritual practices are designed to invite the Lord in. Here are some of the ways in which His presence as a result of worship changes us.

Worship joins us to the Lord. External worship by itself does not join us to the Lord, but external worship as a sincere reflection of our intention to live a good life does (AR 160). "The purpose of all worship is communication with heaven, and by it conjunction of the Lord with a human being" (AC 10436e). Even when worship feels like going through the motions, we are still turning to the Lord, and that turning joins us to Him.

The Lord arranges our heart and mind for the better. When we let Him in, the Lord effortlessly and quickly arranges our thoughts and affections (AC 5705). "When the Lord is present, His very presence arranges everything into order" (AC 5703). This organization of our spirits may be more significant than we expect:

> By external worship internal things are aroused, and by means of external worship external things are kept holy so as to enable internal ones to flow in. Furthermore, people are endowed with concepts by this means, and are made ready to receive celestial things, and also have states of holiness conferred on them, though they are not conscious of this. (AC 1618)

This passage offers a long list of benefits, a list that is noteworthy because we are not consciously aware of much of it. Engaging in various external forms of worship appears to be like a spiritual exercise routine; it starts a chain of events that make unseen changes in us. In time we will feel joy, peace, a sense of purpose, a stronger conscience. But even when we feel nothing, we can know the Lord is making lasting changes for the better.

The Lord protects us. Each spiritual practice the Lord tells us to do is designed to bring His presence into our lives and so to offer protection. The Lord overcomes the hells in our temptations "simply by [His] presence" because the hells cannot stand to be in the presence of the Lord (AC 8137).

Knowing that the Lord's presence offers protection changes the way we can think of spiritual conflict. We do not have to overcome our evils. Rather, we flee from evils as much as we can, and we turn to the Lord as fully as we can. His presence causes hell to flee from us.

Our Actions Create a Vessel for Internal Qualities

External spiritual practices can seem superficial compared to the deeper spiritual practices, and in a way they are. They are like the clothing on the body that protects it from the elements (TCR 55). True charity allows the Lord to create a healthy body; external spiritual practices clothe and protect that body so that in can survive. The Lord also speaks of those external practices as the vessels that contain the inner qualities (AE 126; AC 10546). Liquid without a container is not very useful. These practices are an important component of spiritual living because they clothe, protect, and support our deeper efforts.

In the light of these benefits, it becomes easier to see why these practices can be hard to do: The hells are not simply going to let us develop them without a fight. We might even say these practices are valuable *because* the hells inspire so much resistance to our doing them.

We Grow Gradually

As we've seen, the Lord says that we are supposed to engage in spiritual practices. That seems to lead to the corollary that if we are not going to church, reading the Word, praying, and the like, then we're not good people. While it's true that good people do engage in spiritual practices, the corollary is dangerous; we are all a work in progress. Our true spiritual character is determined by our willingness to look to the Lord, shun evils as sins, and serve others sincerely in our daily work. Those internal activities are the tipping point, the gateway to heaven. What we will find is that the more we do them, the more we will want to do some of the other external spiritual practices. Our challenge is the same as any natural one we face: Rather than trying to fix every issue in our lives at once, we need to pick one spiritual practice to work on. Then in time we could add another. The Lord pays more attention to the incremental progress in our lives than to the work still to be done.

FROM ANOTHER ANGLE: DAILY PRACTICES

Another way of exploring what spiritual practices we should focus on is to consider what the Lord tells us to do every day. We do many things in our lives only when we feel moved to, but other actions are so important to us that we build them into the fabric of our lives as a ritual or practice. Some are external, such as showing up to work on time because we want to keep our job. Others are deeper, such as making time for loved ones even in busy periods because we want them to know we value the relationship.

The Lord tells us about certain spiritual practices that should be daily events, events that we ritualize. Here is a list of things that the Lord tells us to do on a daily basis. Interestingly, it looks a lot like the lists we've seen so far:

- We should seek, or turn to, the Lord daily (Is 58:2, Ps 72:15; AC 2405:8).
- We should repent daily (Luke 9:23; AC 6309, 8391; HD 163; TCR 539).
- We should serve others daily in some useful way (Life 114; Char 158).

Those are the three core practices of charity (p. 5). The other things the Lord tells us to do daily (or weekly for church) are the external signs of charity:

- We are to keep the Sabbath holy (weekly), meaning that we are to worship the Lord on the Sabbath (AC 1798:3, 5135:3).
- We should pray daily (Ps 88:9, 72:15, 61:8; AC 5135:3; SE 361).
- We should praise, thank, and sing to the Lord daily (Ps 145:2, 104:33, 34:1-3, 70:4, 71:8, 61:8, 92:1,2; AC 1798).
- We should read the Word every day, even as children (AE 803:2; see also HD 149; HH 598). Angels read the Word every day, and by implication so should we (AE 1024:2; SE 5618).
- We should meditate (or reflect) on what the Word teaches daily (Josh 1:8; Ps 1:2, 119:97; see also AC 8391).

This second list is much the same as the list of core signs of charity: worship, prayer, reading the Word, and thinking about spiritual matters.

The Lord tells us to spend time on these eight practices, and He emphasizes this by telling us to do them not just sometimes but daily. The Lord places a high premium on our doing these spiritual activities!

The Lord says these practices are important, but many other things in our lives also seem important and pressing. We might wonder how necessary it is to make spiritual practices a priority in our lives, especially the five external ones. The challenging answer to this question is that we make time for what is important to us. In a chapter in *Heaven and Hell* titled, "It is not so hard to lead the life that leads to heaven as people believe," the Lord tells us that to get to heaven, all we have to do is keep the commandments (HH 528-535). And this includes attending worship (HH 531). The point of this chapter is that spiritual living is not so hard, and going to church is included in the list of activities that are easy enough for us to find time and energy to engage in.

As we saw above, these spiritual practices are not just insurance against future harm; they are more like the foundation to our house, something we cannot do without, neither in the here and now, nor in the future. When we think of these spiritual practices as a foundation for our spiritual life, we can see the value in making time for them.

The Lord does indicate that there can be times in our lives when the cares of the world will intrude on our ability to do these practices intentionally. People who are too busy with making a living sometimes do not have the time or ability to reflect about spiritual matters (SS 59; TCR 354:3; AE 787:4). Many people have seasons and times when this is so, and the Lord knows when we're swamped. But if this becomes a normal state, month in and month out, we need to stop and reflect on why. Maybe we need to say no to some good things so that we can say yes to something more important.

PRACTICE BECOMES HABIT; HABIT BECOMES CHARACTER

> *Action comes first, then the desire for it in the person's will follows. For when we are led by our understanding to carry out any action, we are at length led by our will to do it, till at last we have taken it on as an action performed habitually. (AC 4353:3)*

The goal of spiritual living is for good actions to flow spontaneously from us, which is what a true good habit does (AC 3203:1-2). Yet whenever the Lord tells us to do something, at first we have to compel ourselves to do it. We engage in the action knowing we don't really want to just yet but trusting that if we persevere the Lord will make us want to. It is notable that the Lord lays out a sequence of steps, from self-compulsion, to doing something because we want to do it, to doing it as a habit. We often talk about habits in the context of bad habits that we unconsciously fall into. But here a habit is something so ingrained in us that we don't have to choose to do it any more but are instead moved by an unconscious, even spontaneous, choice (see SE 4221). We tend to think of a conscious decision as the end goal, yet it is this habitual unconscious behavior that becomes part of our identity and of the heredity that we pass on to our children (AC 3469, 2300).

Habits make it easy to do what is good (TCR 563). The goal of spiritual living is to develop an internal orientation to doing what we know the Lord wants. The Lord gives us a sequence to follow to get us there, and establishing habits of spiritual practice is an end goal of that sequence.

Each of us is on a journey of doing these internal and external spiritual practices, first because we know they are right, then because we want to, and finally because doing them is who we are, and we could no more avoid doing them than we could avoid sleeping, or eating, or breathing.

PART 1
INTERNAL SPIRITUAL PRACTICES

It is impossible to worship the Lord except from charity. Worship stemming from faith that has no connection with charity is not possible, because it is worship solely of the lips and not of the heart. (AC 440)

We turn now to the three deeper spiritual practices that are at the heart of New Church teaching: turning to the Lord, shunning evils as sins, and serving others. These are the most important spiritual practices, and the Lord put us in this world to give us the opportunity to develop them.

Because they are so important, the Lord has given us a lot of teaching about them, and on the whole they are easier to accept as important activities for us to engage in. The following three chapters offer a summary of the teachings about them. I would recommend reading these chapters carefully and applying each of them before moving on to the chapters that follow. Once we are trying to live an internal, spiritual life, then the external practices the Lord tells us to do will take on new and powerful meaning.

Another possible approach is to choose one internal and one external practice to focus on. Since the external practices support the internal ones, it might actually be easier to succeed if you are doing one of each.

Turn to the Lord

To know the Lord is the most important of all doctrinal matters, or its first and last. (AE 45)

OUR IDEA OF GOD

Thus says Jehovah: "Let not the wise person glory in his wisdom, let not the mighty person glory in his might, nor let the rich person glory in his riches. But let him who glories glory in this, that he understands and knows Me, that I am Jehovah, exercising mercy, judgment, and justice in the earth. For in these I delight," says Jehovah. (Jer 9:23, 24)

When we are trying to live a spiritual life, we may want to leap right into taking action. The Lord asks us to focus first on something else that will make a big difference in our ability to be successful; He wants us to understand who He is so that we can experience His love and turn to Him as the source of strength and guidance in our effort to become better people:

> The very first thing a person needs to do is to acknowledge that the Lord is the Savior of the world; for unless a person acknowledges this, no one can receive any truth or good at all from heaven, or therefore receive faith from there. (AC 10083:5)

This can be challenging to do because we have to quiet our minds against everyday concerns and stretch ourselves to think about things we normally do not.

Consider how valuable it would be for us to have a clear image of a God who loves us, who is always present, who offers us all the wisdom we need to navigate the challenges of life, and whose power we can draw on to fight our spiritual battles. We could love such a God in return, and we could feel safe. By way of analogy, think of someone who has never met their mother or father. What would it be like for that person to be given a picture of their parent, to be given a video of that parent speaking, especially speaking to them about their hopes and dreams for their child, or better still, to actually meet that parent?

Because thinking about the Lord stretches us, and because understanding Him is so important, I recommend reading this chapter more slowly and reflectively than the other chapters. Investing time and energy in understanding the Lord is worth the effort.

Just how important is our idea of God? "The whole of theology hangs on it like a chain on its anchor point," and "the idea everyone has of God determines his place in the heavens" (TCR 163; DLW 13). That's pretty fundamental, so fundamental that we might dismiss it, just as we don't spend time thinking about the importance of our breathing, or the beating of our heart.

It is important to have a clear idea of the Lord, both of His abstract qualities of love and wisdom, of His mercy and justice, and also of how these qualities show themselves in a human form that is a perfect vessel for them. Understanding the infinite God of the universe is not easy! Our finite human minds do not readily come to an understanding of our Lord; we have to work at it. So as you read this chapter, be gentle with yourself if you struggle with some of the teachings you find. The Lord has revealed Himself so we can feel His joy and peace. Learn what you can, and resolve to keep learning and serving. The Lord will guide you. Maybe a good approach to the teachings that are harder to understand would be saying, like the father with the demon-possessed child, "Lord I believe; help my unbelief" (Mark 9:24). This powerful image of how the Lord wants us to see Him might help you on your journey:

> This new church is the crown of all the churches that have up to now existed on the earth because it will worship one visible God, in whom is the invisible God, like the soul in the body. In this way and no other is the conjunction of God with people possible, because people are natural and so think in a natural fashion; and conjunction must take place in their thought and so in the desires of their love. This happens when people think of God as a person.... Connecting with a visible God is like seeing a person in the air or on the sea, opening His arms and inviting you into His embrace. All conjunction of God with people must also be a reciprocal joining of people with God, and this second joining is not possible except with a visible God. (TCR 787)

When Our Ideas of God Go Wrong

> *No more shall everyone teach his neighbor, and everyone his brother, saying, "Know the Lord," for they all shall know Me. (Jer 31:34)*

One of the hardest aspects about coming to understand and know the Lord is that we've never seen Him or met Him. Because of this, we can come up with ideas about who He is, sometimes wildly incorrect ones. Incorrect ways we picture God, such as the following, can make it hard for us to relate to Him:

- God is "up there" somewhere at a distance and is not immediately present in our lives.
- God is perfect, so our flaws and imperfections seem impossibly impure and disconnected from God. How could God ever relate to us?
- God is the speaker of truth, and truth judges us and everyone else harshly.

- God is a source of love apart from truth, so all actions and motives are forgiven or overridden, and our actions have no consequences.
- If God has all power, then all things that happen must somehow be God's will. This means that God is the agent of all the bad things and seeming punishments that occur in the world.
- Since God is by definition fair, anything bad that happens to us is our fault or was "meant to be."
- Dividing God up into three persons, whether in our words on in our unspoken ideas, leads us to an internal belief that there is no God, except nature.
- Since we cannot see God, it is hard to believe that He even exists.
- We want to turn to concrete images so we can relate to God, and we place too much power and importance on a picture or statue (idolatry) or on a place (as if God is present only in church, for instance).
- Because we don't see God interacting with us, we can think that God created the world but that now we are on our own.
- Humans have messed up, and God is angry because of it. Unless we do things just right to appease Him, we are going to suffer His wrath. We have to be perfect to earn God's approval.
- Since we can't really picture God, and we certainly can't picture how Father, Son, and Holy Spirit are all somehow one God, we end up giving up and having no real idea of God.

It seems that we humans tend to err in two ways: We make God invisible and unknowable, or we get so specific in our thinking that we make God overly human; we create God in our image rather than the reverse.

Each incorrect idea of who God is can lead to painful or unhelpful ideas about how to interact with Him, and these ideas limit our choices and our happiness. By developing a more accurate idea of Him, we become able to receive God's love and wisdom more fully and wholeheartedly.

The Divine Human—A Perfect Yet Visible God

> *"All power has been given to Me in heaven and on earth." (Matt 28:18)*

> *All Divine worship begins in the Divine Human; and the Divine Human is what one is to worship, for by worshiping this one worships the Divine Itself, no thought of whom can otherwise be formed. And if no such thought can be formed, there can be no communion with Him either. (AC 6674:4)*

The best way to develop useful ideas of God is to see Him as both Divine and Human. Many people can agree on the basic qualities of God: God is infinite, all-powerful, all-knowing, the epitome of love and of wisdom, the creator and source of all blessings. By themselves, these qualities are vague in two ways. First, they create in our minds an incomprehensible being, much like The Force from *Star Wars*, a pervasive presence that we can surrender to but that we cannot know, love, or interact with. Second, words like power, love, and wisdom are open to many interpretations. While we can agree that God is all-loving, unless we have a real understanding of what that love looks like, we tend to create God in our own image, endowing Him with qualities we would like in a Divine being.

If we don't have clear images that support and give reality to our concept of God, that concept tends to be "the figment of a fanciful imagination" (ML 66; see also AC 4733:1-2, 7091). Having no image of Him leads to "ill-formed and sketchy notions resulting from each person's own ideas" (AC 4075:3). This is why the Lord gave us an image of Himself by being born on earth and why He said to Philip, "He who has seen me has seen the Father" (John 14:9).

Some people find the idea of picturing God, especially picturing Him in any detail, alarming. They fear limiting God with an inaccurate picture. I understand this, and I would still encourage us to try to picture the Lord. An abstract idea is an inaccurate one. By concretizing our idea of God over time, we force ourselves to move beyond vague generalities to specifics and so to think more about the Lord than we might otherwise.

It is true that *all* our ideas of God are limited and imperfect. We're not going to "get it right" in the sense of gaining a perfect idea of God. By developing a picture of God, we will find that we can have a more accurate and complete idea Him. Instead of limiting our idea of Him, a true mental picture enhances it. Just below we will explore some ways of forming those images.

A final thought is that we don't need to get overly precise. The Lord does not require us to have a clear image of His hair and eye color, for instance. For some people that would be too specific. Our challenge is to have at least some mental image that contains the deeper ideas we have of Him, just as our mental pictures of loved ones support and contain our ideas of them.

How Might We Develop a Picture of the Lord?

> *The earth shall be full of the knowledge of Jehovah, as the waters cover the sea. (Is 11:9)*

Since it is clear that we need to have some mental image of the Lord, we now turn to how to develop one. The starting point is that Jehovah, the infinite God who created us, was born on earth as Jesus Christ. He took on a finite mind and body from Mary and perfected them. Jesus Christ is the embodiment (literally) of the infinite God, the perfect manifestation of love and wisdom in human form.

We have to make sure that we can picture in the Lord the qualities we know to be in God. Here are some quotations followed by questions to help you develop that picture:

- "The Lord's human, after it was glorified or made Divine, cannot be thought of as human, but as the Divine love in human form" (AC 4735:2). What would Divine love in human form look like? "And when Jesus went out He saw a great multitude; and He was moved with compassion for them, and healed their sick" (Matt 14:14).
- We are told that "the face of the Lord is mercy, peace, and every good" (AC 9293). What would that face look like? "These things I have spoken to you, that in Me you may have peace. In the world you will have tribulation; but be of good cheer, I have overcome the world" (John 16:33).
- The hand represents power, and love has power through wisdom (ML 21; TCR 748). What would hands that have infinite power to protect look like? When Peter tried to walk on water toward the Lord and started to sink, we read, "And immediately Jesus stretched out His hand and caught him, and said to him, 'O you of little faith, why did you doubt?'" (Matt 14:31).
- Eyes also represent wisdom coming from love (AC 9936:4). What would eyes of infinite wisdom and love look like? When Jesus met the rich, young ruler, we read, "Then Jesus, looking at him, loved him, and said to him, 'One thing you lack: Go your way, sell whatever you have and give to the poor, and you will have treasure in heaven; and come, take up the cross, and follow Me'" (Mark 10:21).
- We are taught that mercy is love that is grieving when it sees those it loves in states of pain (AC 5480). What would that mercy look like on the face of God? On Palm Sunday the Lord rode into Jerusalem. "Now as He drew near, He saw the city and wept over it, saying, 'If you had known, even you, especially in this your day, the things that make for your peace! But now they are hidden from your eyes'" (Luke 19:41-42).

The human form is an expression of the human spirit. When we think about love, it has meaning when we think about how human beings express it. And since we are created in the Lord's image, we think of His Divine love by thinking about how He expresses it in His Divine Humanity.

These broad concepts are useful foundations for an idea of the Lord, but part of us wants specific images to help us develop that idea. Only once in Scripture does the Lord give us a specific description of Himself. This happens when He appears to John on the Isle of Patmos (Rev 1), and we're told that He looks "like the Son of Man" (i.e., like Jesus did on earth). John goes on to give us images that are clearly symbolic: "His head and hair were white like wool, as white as snow, and

His eyes like a flame of fire; His feet were like fine brass, as if refined in a furnace, and His voice as the sound of many waters. He had in His right hand seven stars, out of His mouth went a sharp two-edged sword, and His countenance was like the sun shining in its strength" (Rev 1:14-16). This description is similar to the image of the Lord when He was transfigured while on earth (Matt 17:1-13; AE 64). That is one way we could think of Him.

Another way is to think of Jesus Christ walking on earth. What would a person who lived two thousand years ago in Israel have looked like? Likely He'd have had straight dark hair, a beard, olive skin, and a Middle Eastern appearance. Likely He'd not have been as tall as we are today. We're told that when He appears to people on other planets and is described by them, those from our planet who saw Him on earth say that that's how He looked on earth (EU 40; SE 3292). We might say that the body the Lord glorified on earth truly is His body, the one we are supposed to think of. Yet it is notable that the Lord chose not to give us any description of Himself in Scripture, as if tying our mental image of Him to one specific picture would not be useful.

Even though having a mental image of the Lord is important, we can wonder how important the specific details of His appearance are. "The Lord appears to each individual person in a way suited to the kind of person they are, for this is suited to the way the person receives the Lord" (AC 6832:2). Given that each of us knows and lives different truths, it seems reasonable to assume that the Lord will appear to each of us a bit differently. Perhaps the specific details and factual "correctness" of our mental images are not very important. What is important is that we have a mental image that is a vessel for holding our deeper concepts of the Lord. For some people that image may be very general, such as a silhouetted figure of a person.

Some people have said that they struggle to have any image of the Lord, but they can easily hear His voice, as it were, or feel His arms holding them. While the language of the Doctrines focuses on visual imagery, it seems likely that bringing any of the senses into play would be helpful.

Whatever we do, our goal needs to be to develop a mental image of Jesus Christ as our God. When we pray and have the Lord in our mind's eye (DLW 129), that image needs to be of the same Person who walked on earth and perfected His Humanity. The details of that image may vary from person to person because we all create images that reflect the specific truths and affections that are most important to us. But they should be images of that one God, Jesus Christ.

One way of supporting these images and of filling them with qualities of the Lord is to read the New Testament with the intention of learning more about what the Lord is like (see SS 21). How does the Lord feel about those who are lost and hurting? He ate with sinners and tax collectors (Matt 9:9-13). How does He act with sinners? He drives out those who intentionally do evil, such as the moneychangers (Matt 21:12-13), and offers forgiveness and a path forward to those who repent, such as the woman caught in adultery (John 8:2-11). How does He respond to those who betray Him? To Judas He said, "Friend, why have you come?" (Matt 26:50), and on the cross He said, "Father, forgive them, for they do not know what they do" (Luke 23:34). By thinking about and exploring the stories of the New Testament this way, we not only develop our mental image of the Lord, but we also fill that image with rich and powerful concepts of who the Lord is and what it feels like to love Him and to be loved by Him.

SEEING THE LORD'S DEEPER QUALITIES

> *Then the sign of the Son of Man will appear in heaven, and then all the tribes of the earth will mourn, and they will see the Son of Man coming on the clouds of heaven with power and great glory. (Matt 24:30)*

I have emphasized the need to create images of the Lord in part because there is a lot of teaching about this but also because many people in the New Church have expressed that it is difficult to picture Him. However, the point of mental images is to allow us to focus on the deeper qualities that they embody.

As we have already seen, we gain this deeper view by turning to the Lord in His Word. This is the meaning of seeing "the Son of Man coming in the clouds of heaven with power and great glory." This is a prophecy of the Second Coming of the Lord. He did not come back in the flesh, but instead He has allowed us to see Him in a new way. The Son of Man is the Lord; the clouds are the literal teachings of the Word, unclear images of the powerful truths that lie within; and the power and great glory are the insights the Lord gives into the inner meaning of the Word (AC 49:4). We see the Lord when we acknowledge in our "hearts by love and faith" what we see in the Word (AC 6895:2).

We see the Lord's face through the Divine truths that come from Him (AC 10569:6, 9297:2). Think, for instance, about how much we learn about the Lord by coming to understand the laws of Divine Providence, the nature of the spiritual world, or true married love. This reflects our experience that everything new we learn about a person and about what they value and do offers a window into their spirit.

An important teaching about seeing the Lord is that "those who receive enlightenment when they read the Word see the Lord…. They see Him solely in the Word and in no other writing whatever" (AC 9411). Nothing else is able to contain the perfect, holy presence of the Lord. This means that we need to be regularly turning to the Word to create more vessels in our minds that can contain an idea of the Lord.

SEEK THE LORD

> *To believe in the Lord is to turn directly to Him and have confidence that He will save. (AR 553:2)*

This chapter is about turning to the Lord. In order to turn to Him, we have to know who He is and come to hold an image of Him in our minds. These require that we focus our minds. But even more than that, we have to open our hearts; we have to be searching Him out, similar to the way that people who are falling in love strive to get to know each other better. Time and again in Scripture the Lord talks about the need to seek Him out. As the following passages show, the spiritual practices we are exploring are the pathways the Lord has laid out for seeking Him.

We are to seek Him out from a sincere desire

One thing I have desired of the Lord, that will I seek: That I may dwell in the house of the Lord all the days of my life, to behold the beauty of the Lord, and to inquire in His temple. (Ps 27:4)

We are to seek Him out in worship and prayer

Oh, give thanks to the Lord! Call upon His name; make known His deeds among the peoples! Sing to Him, sing psalms to Him; talk of all His wondrous works! Glory in His holy name; let the hearts of those rejoice who seek the Lord! Seek the Lord and His strength; seek His face evermore! (Ps 105:1-4)

We are to seek to know Him (presumably through His Word)

Yet they seek Me daily, and delight to know My ways. (Is 58:2)

And most importantly, we are to seek Him by repenting

Those who seek the Lord shall not lack any good thing.... Keep your tongue from evil, and your lips from speaking deceit. Depart from evil and do good; seek peace and pursue it. (Ps 34:10, 13-14)

Seek the Lord while He may be found, call upon Him while He is near. Let the wicked forsake his way, and the unrighteous man his thoughts; let him return to the Lord, and He will have mercy on him; and to our God, for He will abundantly pardon. (Is 55:6-7)

The Lord is reality; He is present with each of us. Our task is to invite Him in. By ourselves, spiritual living is impossible, but not with God. With God in our lives, when we intentionally turn to Him, all good things are possible (see Matt 19:26).

THE BEST KIND OF TURNING TO THE LORD

The goal of spiritual living is to turn to the Lord constantly, no matter what we are doing. One passage describes this idea beautifully:

> People who receive and possess faith are constantly mindful of the Lord. This is so even when they are thinking or talking about something other than Him, or else when they are carrying out their public, private, or family duties, though they are not directly conscious of their mindfulness of the Lord while carrying them out. Indeed that mindfulness of the Lord present in those who possess faith governs their whole being, but that which governs their whole being is not noticed by them except when they turn their thought specifically to that matter. (AC 5130)

When we are in the stream of Providence, that stream is constantly carrying us along to what is happy and good, even when we are not aware of it (AC 8478:4). We develop an ongoing and constant interaction with the Lord, trusting in His will and bowing to the gentle urges, redirections, and insights He is offering us all the time. This living presence of the Lord is the goal of life and the source of happiness.

PULLING IT TOGETHER

Our idea of the Lord is at the heart of our ability to live happy and fulfilled spiritual lives, and it is at the heart of our spiritual practice. In order to turn to Him, we need to know who He is.

To know Him we need to know His inner qualities of love and wisdom, not just in broad, abstract terms but in the real way that we know the inner qualities of those we love. This requires study and effort, particularly because the hells try to stop us from thinking about Him (AC 7118).

We also need to have a mental image of the Lord within which our ideas about Him can rest. His qualities have meaning for us only insofar as we can picture in our mind's eye His interaction with us and with the universe. When we think of God as Human, and even more when we think of Jesus Christ as God, we bring infinite love, wisdom, and power into a comprehensible form that we can interact with and love. This idea of a Human God is encapsulated in a passage quoted earlier in this chapter: "Connecting with a visible God is like seeing a person in the air or on the sea, opening His arms and inviting you into His embrace" (TCR 787). When we can take the qualities we know to be in God and see them embodied in Jesus Christ, we can experience His presence and settle into the warmth and protection of His embrace.

The most important way we come to know the Lord is by turning to Him and doing His will. When we decide that what is important to the Lord is important to us, we allow Him to change us from the inside out, and we become increasingly aware of His living presence in our hearts, minds, and lives.

ACTIVITIES AND QUESTIONS

1. Which qualities of the Lord that are particularly important to you?

2. What verses from Scripture about the Lord speak strongly to you?

3. What is your mental picture of the Lord?
   a. Some people struggle with a mental image but can hear His voice or feel Him holding them. That's a good start because it brings the senses into play.
   b. One way to help with this is to think about the qualities of the Lord that are important to you. (See question 1.) If you really appreciate the Lord's love and compassion, what would perfect love and compassion look like on a face that is looking at you? If you value His power, what might His hands look like? Try to embody His inner qualities in a mental image.

4. Read through the New Testament with the prayerful desire to notice the stories that bring the Lord vividly alive in your mind's eye. What images do they create? What qualities are depicted in them?

5. Commit to one or more ways to seek the Lord in your life. Some possible suggestions:
   a. Pray daily, possibly more.
   b. Read the Word—Old Testament, New Testament, or Heavenly Doctrines. Focus on what the stories and passages say about who the Lord is and what He does for us.
   c. Make attending worship a regular pattern in your life.
   d. Talk to others about their idea of the Lord. Each of us has a limited concept of the Lord, so sharing our insights can help us expand our idea.
   e. Meditate in the presence of the Lord. ("Be still and know that I am God.")

6. Find a time in the week when you can slow down enough to think for a little while about the Lord and your life. What do you need to give up in order to make this space?

Repent: The Path to Joy and Peace

*I would rather be a doorkeeper in the house of my God than dwell in
the tents of wickedness. For Jehovah God is a sun and shield; Jehovah
will give grace and glory. No good thing will He withhold from those
who walk in integrity. (Ps 84:10, 11)*

People who seek to become spiritual want to be considerate, kind, and loving people who act with integrity toward others. Yet we are not inherently thoughtful
about others' needs. A child, by instinct, seeks to fulfill his or her needs and has
to be taught to behave differently. We have to work hard to push away our selfish
desires and instincts.

The steps of repentance offer a pathway from that instinctual regard for self to
becoming loving people. That involves looking at what is not good in ourselves
with the goal of opening ourselves up to joy and peace.

GUIDING PRINCIPLES ABOUT REPENTANCE

*To look to God in one's life means simply to think that this or that evil
is a sin against God, and for that reason not to do it. (DP 20)*

The most general teaching about repentance is that we should shun evils as sins
against God. This means that we should shun evils because they are spiritually
wrong and harmful, not because we have decided that shunning them is a good
idea. "If people do not shun evils from a religious principle, because they are sins
and against God, the lusts of evil with their delights still remain like polluted waters
dammed up or stagnant" (DP 117).

Although we recognize that the Lord does the primary work, we have an active
part to play. We are supposed to shun evils as if from ourselves (DP 116), meaning
that we are supposed to do the work as if from our own power, all the while acknowledging that the Lord is the one who truly gives us the power. Only when we
act as if from ourselves in our external actions can the Lord purify us from within
(DP 119, 120).

The benefit of turning to the Lord as we try to change is that we enlist the
power and wisdom of an infinite and loving God. All too often we can feel lost and
alone in our spiritual struggles. Turning to the Lord brings Him into our efforts.

How Often Should We Repent?

We can think about approaching repentance in two ways. If repenting is the process of turning to the Lord to remove evil and do what is good, it is something we should be doing all the time. The Lord teaches that spiritual people do the work of repentance daily (Luke 9:23; AC 6309). It is easy to imagine doing a daily check-in each evening to see how we did and to ask the Lord for help in areas of weakness. Even if we do this just once a week or twice a month, we will notice a change (Lord 97).

We can also think of repentance as a big project we take on occasionally, "once or twice a year" (AR 224:6) or "at recurring seasons" in preparation for Holy Supper (TCR 530). This level of repentance seems more like a deep spring cleaning compared to the daily process of keeping things tidy. Daily repentance maintains what the deep cleaning accomplishes, but unless we engage in that deeper examination, we may never uncover important issues we need to address.

THE STEPS OF REPENTANCE

The Lord offers several lists of steps of repentance. We often use this list of four:

1) Examine yourself.
2) Recognize and acknowledge an evil desire.
3) Pray to the Lord for help and the power to resist.
4) Begin a new life (TCR 528).

We will go through what each of these four steps means.

1) Examine Yourself

> The things that have become habitual, that is, familiar, cease to be recognized by a person as being present in him, although they are present. (AC 7398)

In order to repent, we need to see what is going on in our lives. The Lord says more about this step than about the rest combined. Perhaps that's because the raw honesty of looking at our lives to see the underlying reality is not easy. Sometimes we hide from reality, and sometimes we become dramatic and condemn everything about ourselves in the name of being realistic. Neither of these is true self-examination.

The purpose of self-examination is to study our actions to see what is out of line with the Lord's teaching. But it is more than that. We also need to explore the motives and thoughts that drive our actions. This is because an action that may seem good can be bad if done for the wrong reasons, and an action that may seem bad can be acceptable to the Lord in the right context.

The point of self-examination is to find a specific evil that is active in our lives that we want to remove. An excellent way to do this is to consider what we would do if all rules and consequences were suspended (TCR 566). What would you do if you had a week to act with total impunity—a spiritual get-out-of-jail-free card?

The goal of examining yourself is to find the issue in your life that is most threatening to your spiritual well-being. Here are a few things to consider as you do some self-examination.

- What are the general trends in your life? Ongoing problems tend to be more important than something that comes up once in a while.
- Look for the problems which seem the most spiritually damaging (TCR 509).
- As a general rule, don't work on more than one or two at a time (TCR 566:2), or you will get overwhelmed and fail.
- Turn to the Lord in prayer, asking Him to show you what you need to work on. Over the course of a week, He will likely shine the light on what you need to see.
- Look first for bad things you are actually doing. If you don't find anything significant there, then look for selfish thoughts and desires.
- All evil loves cloak themselves in disguises of respectability, or at least of being justified. Children learn this early: "I only hit her because she was teasing me!" Be on the lookout for justifications and lies that prevent a destructive action or motive from coming to light.
- Don't worry about good things you are doing for mixed motives. Focus first on the genuinely bad things; likely there will be enough of those.

Here are a few thoughts about the technique, or how to go about actually doing self-examination.

- Ask the Lord to show you your worst problem over the next few days. You will probably find that whatever you need to work on will come up repeatedly, in your thoughts if not in your actions.
- You need time to reflect on your life when doing self-examination. Choose a time when you have a bit more space in your schedule.
- Read the Word or sing songs that bring you close to the Lord. His presence shines a light on your life.
- Don't spend too long on this step. You won't get to the bottom of everything you need to work on in your life. Find one meaningful issue and work on it.

By holding some of these ideas in your mind, you will likely find that the Lord can shine a light on your life that gives you clarity about the next thing to work on.

2) Recognize and Acknowledge an Evil Pattern

Once we see an evil in ourselves, the next step is to acknowledge it. There is a difference between seeing something and acknowledging it. We see with our intellect, but we acknowledge from the heart. We acknowledge an evil when we accept that we did it on purpose. We've all hurt people without being aware of it. When we see what we've done, we apologize and move on with no need to repent. But evils we intended are something we need to take deeper responsibility for.

Another part of recognizing an evil is coming to see more fully the consequences of its presence. Our own particular evils are like intimate friends. We may, from long familiarity, overlook things we have become accustomed to. Over time we learn to see these "as sweet drugs that kill, or as apparently beautiful flowers that carry poison in them" (Char 2). And we need to see how the particular poison has acted to cause harm. When we recognize this, we can take responsibility for our lives and choices because we move from a broad awareness of an evil to seeing its specific damage in our lives and in the lives of those around us. This opens a door for us to move on to the next step.

3) Open the Door: Pray for Help and the Power to Resist

> *"Behold, I stand at the door and knock. If anyone hears My voice and opens the door, I will come in to him and dine with him, and he with Me." (Rev 3:20)*

The first two steps—discovering the evil and acknowledging it—involve seeing what is in our lives. The next two steps shift our attention toward doing something about it. When we ask the Lord for help, we change our focus. Even though we are not acting yet, we are seeking help so we can act. We acknowledge that we face an evil we cannot overcome alone. There is much more to say about prayer which will come in a later chapter.

When we ask the Lord for help, we need ask only for today. After all, the only time we'll ever need strength from the Lord to follow through is right now. When tomorrow comes, we will need to ask for that strength again—right now. "Give us this day our daily bread," the Lord's prayer says. "Therefore do not worry about tomorrow, for tomorrow will worry about its own things. Sufficient for the day is its own evil" (Matt 6:24). The Alcoholics Anonymous (AA) motto, "One day at a time," is a wise one.

4) Begin a New Life

With step four, we aim to change our actions. Previous to this we have learned what the challenge is and have prepared ourselves for combat. Now we stop doing the selfish behavior. I want to emphasize that it is ineffective to skip over any of the first three steps. People do that all the time, then find that they don't have staying power when it gets hard. The purpose of those first three steps is to give us a firm foundation for this last crucial step. If we've prepared properly, we'll find that we can be much more successful with this step.

This does not mean that we will *feel* like stopping. Another AA slogan comes into play here: "Fake it till you make it." Spiritual growth requires us to act certain ways when we may not feel like it and to keep doing so until eventually we want to do what's right. But that takes time. As we saw earlier, "Action comes first, then the desire for it in our will follows. For when we are led by our understanding to carry out any action, we are at length led by our will to do it, till at last we have taken it on as an action performed habitually" (AC 4353:3).

There is a hidden benefit to self-compulsion. Although it can at first feel freeing and energizing to make a new start, that feeling will not last. What carries us through is the willingness to compel ourselves even when we do not feel like it. When we compel ourselves, we assert our freedom more strongly than at any other time. This is because there is an interior freedom that comes from choosing in our spirits to do what is right even when we do not feel like it (AC 1937:5). The Lord is deeply present in this choice.

THE REWARD OF SHUNNING EVIL

The reward of shunning evil is that to the extent we do it, we receive the opposite good. That is why we fight:

> As far as evils are removed, so far goods enter. That this is so can be seen by a person from natural light alone, for when lustfulness is removed chastity enters; when intemperance is removed temperance enters; when deceit is removed sincerity enters; when hatred and the delight of revenge are removed love and the delight of love and friendship enter; and so in other cases. The reason is that the Lord enters, and heaven with Him, so far as people from the Word abstain from doing evils, since they then abstain from them from the Lord. (AE 790:6)

The reason we spend so much of our lives fighting what feel like the same evils over and over is that each time we fight, it is against a slightly different version of that evil. And when we conquer that particular evil we gain the opposite good. This is the Lord's method for continually giving us good things, which is His great desire.

Pulling It Together

We can see that the pathway towards being who and what we really want to be begins with repentance. All of us have many hopes and dreams for what our lives can become and how we can make a difference in the world. We picture the good we can do and be, and we may wish that simply paying attention to the good that we want to accomplish were enough. But the pathway to making our dreams real begins with repentance. Each time we examine ourselves, recognize and acknowledge an evil, pray to the Lord for help, and begin a new life, we allow the Lord to change us. By doing all this because it is what He teaches, we open our spirits to His infinite power, and we receive His tender mercy into our hearts and lives. We will never do anything more important than the steps of repentance; our ability to do everything else we care about depends on doing them.

Activities and Questions

1. Looking back on your life, what evils have you tended toward consistently?

2. When you are by yourself, what negative or self-indulgent thoughts tend to recur frequently?

3. If you were writing a book with yourself as the protagonist, what traits would you portray as your strengths and weaknesses?

4. When you have attempted to change your life in the past, when did it flow easily and when was it hard?

5. What we shun affects the good loves that we develop. What do you value enough that you are willing to do the hard work of rejecting the things that stand in the way of its development?

6. Go through the steps of repentance carefully, and prayerfully, and notice the results. For extra help and specific worksheets, you can go to www.beginanewlife.info.

7. If you are having trouble succeeding by yourself, consider getting help or support from a minister or trusted friend.

Serve Others

Whoever desires to become great among you, let him be your servant.
(Matt 20:26)

We are born for the sole purpose of performing, while we live in the world, a use to the community we are in, and to our neighbor, and in the next life of performing a use in accord with the Lord's good pleasure. (AC 1103)

We come now to the last of the three internal practices: doing good to others. As the quote just above shows, our "sole purpose" is to make a difference by serving others, and everything else we do (turning to the Lord and shunning evils) helps us get there. We need to observe all the external spiritual practices that come later in this book so that we have the insight, strength, and desire to serve the Lord and others. Service to the Lord and others is the ultimate good, the sum of all the parts, the reason for our existence, and the source of our lasting happiness.

This chapter will offer primarily a summary of the principles the Lord saw fit to lay out for us in the chapter on charity in *True Christian Religion*. But first we will explore two principles that can guide our thinking.

The first principle concerns how we think of worship. A common teaching is that "essential divine worship" consists in "a life of love, charity, and faith, in accordance with doctrine" rather than in acts of outward devotion (HH 222; AC 1618). As we have seen and will see again later, this does not mean that outward worship is unimportant or that it is okay to avoid it (AC 1618). What it does mean is that we can go about our daily work as an act of worship, as a way of honoring the Lord through our daily actions.

The second principle is that being useful is what makes us happy. It is common for people to long to be finished with work and to look forward to when they can relax. Yet the Lord teaches that happiness comes from being useful. When some spirits wanted to know about heavenly joy, they were told,

> It is the pleasure of doing something that is of use to oneself and to others, and the pleasure in being useful takes its essence from love and its expression from wisdom. The pleasure in being useful, springing from love through wisdom, is the life and soul of all heavenly joys. (ML 5:3)

This teaching offers a number of insights about the joy of usefulness.

Serving others is heavenly joy. The very act of being useful is pleasurable. We may not always feel this, but delight is inherent in usefulness, as we experience when we take on a needed chore and find quiet satisfaction in accomplishing it, perhaps more than we expected.

Being useful benefits both "oneself and others." While the Lord generally intends that usefulness be rewarding, it is also true that we will at times compel ourselves to do what is useful and take no joy in it. But for self-compulsion to have impact, our inner self will have to take delight in doing good even if the outer self has not yet found that enjoyment.

Our goal, and what makes our service to others heavenly, is to *act from love by means of wisdom*. Clearly that does not always happen. Sometimes we act because we know we should. Sometimes we don't know the wisest way to serve others. When love, wisdom, and usefulness come together, we feel delight in serving others. And even when we do not, the willingness to serve others brings an element of delight that will motivate us from within.

Being useful, then, brings benefit and joy to us and to others. We now turn to the ways in which the Lord tells us to be useful.

THE LORD'S PRIORITIES FOR SERVING OTHERS

In *True Christian Religion (TCR),* where the Lord organizes His teaching about serving others into one chapter, He offers us insight into His priorities about service that can add focus to our own usefulness. Here are some of the main ideas from that chapter in the order in which the Lord presented them. These principles can guide our choices of useful service.

Putting Higher Loves above Lower Ones

There seem to be many more good and useful things to do than there are hours to do them. The Lord offers principles to help us untangle our thinking and decide which opportunities are probably most important. The first two sections in the chapter in TCR have to do with giving priority to the right kinds of love.

The first section explains that there are three underlying loves that drive all our actions: self-love,[1] love for worldly items and concerns, and love of heaven[2] (TCR 394). Each of these loves is, from creation, a heavenly love (DLW 396). But they have to be properly prioritized in us to remain heavenly. When they are in their

---

[1] Self-love in this teaching is defined primarily as "the love of honors, glory, fame, and eminence, [and] also the love of winning and angling for offices, and thus dominating others" (TCR 394). Its focus is the ambition that leads us to do great things or gain control. This love can also be a healthy self-regard that leads us to care for ourselves so that we can serve others (see TCR 406).

[2] "Love of heaven" includes both charity toward the neighbor and love for the Lord.

proper order—love of heaven first, love of the world next, and self-love last—all of them lead us to serve others from love, but when they are out of order, they corrupt us (TCR 395). As we look at our lives, we can ask where we are making choices in favor of lower forms of love at the expense of higher ones, and then reprioritize.

The next section in TCR gives us further clarity about what is most important. It describes the degrees of the neighbor. The basic principle is that the needs of groups of people are more important than the needs of individuals, and the needs of spiritually-focused groups of people are more important still. Here is a composite list of the degrees of the neighbor, in ascending importance: self, individuals around us, communities, our country, the world or human race, the church, the Lord's kingdom,[1] and the Lord (TCR 406-416; Char 72-89; AC 6818-6824).

Each higher degree of the neighbor is more the neighbor than the lower degree. That means that when there is an apparent conflict between two, our allegiance should go to the higher degree of the neighbor. This is why in time of war a soldier leaves his family, whom he loves, to defend his country, or why someone may leave a high-paying job to work for the country or the church at lower pay. And it is why countless people choose to be honest or kind (obeying the Lord or the church's teachings) even when it costs them time or money.

The Lord's introductory message to us about being useful is that we should pay attention to what is most important. When things are in their proper order, they are all good.

Doing Your Job Honestly, Justly, and Faithfully

> *Charity itself is dealing fairly and faithfully in whatever position, business, or work one is engaged in, and with those with whom one comes into contact.* (TCR 422)

New Church teaching radically redefines what "work" means. Many people think of their job[2] as a necessary evil or something to get through so they can put food on the table. The Lord offers a different view, one in which our daily work becomes our primary form of offering service to the world. Rather than thinking of our job as something we do until we have enough money to retire, we can think of it as a daily purpose that can be central to our happiness and the happiness of others.

---

[1] The Lord's kingdom is the universal church throughout the whole world, or all good people who are looking to something more than themselves (TCR 416).

[2] Throughout this section, I use the term "job" broadly to mean our primary area of usefulness, the one we spend most of our waking hours thinking about and engaging in. This may look quite different for different people.

Our goal is to develop the spontaneous desire to serve, and to reject and leave behind the idea of service as mere duty or drudgery (AC 4029-33).[1]

The passage quoted above and others like it use the words fairly, faithfully, honestly, and justly to describe doing our job. These words depict integrity. Another passage describes doing our jobs as a duty we owe to the world (TCR 423). While another passage speaks of doing our work from affection and with delight (Char 158), the Lord does not say that we should start out seeking excitement or fulfillment. We want enjoyment and inspiration, but we have little control over how often these emotions show up. However, whatever job we have, we can choose to act with integrity, and if we do, we will find that the other things come. To quote from a slightly different context, "Seek first the kingdom of God and His justice, and all these things will be added to you" (Matt 6:33; see also TCR 736:3).

Thinking about our work this ways turns it into a spiritual practice: "If we look to the Lord and shun evils as sins, and sincerely, justly, and faithfully perform" the work set before us, we become a form of charity (Char 158; Char 160-172). By contrast, if we are not looking to the Lord and shunning evils, we will not be able to sincerely do our jobs (TCR 423). Our real job, whatever the external tasks may be, involves finding ways to act *spiritually* in our daily service of others. Work is no longer about how many of something we make but instead about how we serve others in making them, or how we don't cut corners in a way that might hurt someone, or that we interact well with coworkers. Work is no longer about how many clients we see but about the kindness and integrity we bring to each visit. Work is not about getting noticed and rewarded but about caring for people's well-being even when no one notices.

Instead of thinking about our job as working on the business we are in, we need to think of it as making others' lives better. On one level, we make their lives better by what we do, but we make a much bigger difference by *how* we do it and the quality of spirit we bring to doing it. We've all been around diligent and dedicated but critical people. They get a lot done, but they are unpleasant to be around, so they are not being particularly useful to the spirits of those around them. Likely we have all been around people whose spirit of compassion and integrity make us want to be better human beings. This is why the real tasks that support our daily effectiveness are the moral and spiritual tasks involved in shunning evils as sins against the Lord. Benefitting the spirits of other people is our real job description.

---

[1] It is a different matter when we compel ourselves. Then we are actually acting in freedom, however we may feel (AC 4031:4).

Good Deeds (Benefactions of Charity)

Doing our jobs honestly, justly, and faithfully is our primary responsibility, but the Lord also lists three other forms of service we should engage in, of which good deeds is the first. Good deeds are acts of kindness to others, apart from our job, that we choose to do "as a matter of free choice and pleasure," and they are regarded by those who receive them simply as kind deeds rather than as obligatory services (TCR 425). Our willingness to stop and notice someone else's need and to put our lives on hold to meet that need makes it a good deed.

Although good deeds are not charity in itself, they perform an important function in the development of charity in us, particularly when we give to the needy. "By acts like these, boys and girls, male and female servants, and simple people of all kinds are initiated into the exercise of charity. These actions are outward acts that lead people to absorb the function of charity. They are its beginnings" (TCR 426:2). In fact, the Lord tells us that regeneration begins with them (AC 3688:3-5), and all future spiritual development rests on and builds on them, along with other teachings drawn from the letter of the Word (AC 5945). So these deeds are important. They are like the unripe fruits from which the ripe fruits of true charity develop (TCR 426:2), which means parents, teachers, and churches need to provide opportunities for the young and uneducated to begin to practice charity. And it would also seem important, with children and those new to the church, to avoid over-focusing on the teachings about being discerning in our charitable deeds because they cannot do this (AC 3688:3). Instead, we should emphasize external good deeds as a key launching point for spiritual living. The church needs to engage in encouraging, and possibly even providing opportunities for, good deeds as an external that supports the deeper life of charity.

As we do these good deeds, we will become aware that we need to practice discernment in how we help people. Undiscerning good deeds, which are those done equally to anyone in need, may actually hurt rather than help because they can give bad people the ability to hurt good people—like feeding a starving thief who then grows strong enough to go out and rob people (TCR 428). A principle that helps us hone our practices is that the good in the neighbor is what is to be loved (HD 86-89). We want to make sure that our kind deeds support the good in the neighbor, not the bad. Much of the time it is easy to decide. For example, no one hesitates to bring a meal to a family suffering from the loss of a loved one or to help someone whose car has broken down. At other times it is harder to know how to help, and we will need to exercise some thought and caution rather than simply following our hearts.

Duties or Obligations Arising from Charity

While good deeds often arise out of a sense of compassion, other forms of charity arise out of an awareness of obligation. Over and above our daily occupations, by virtue of being citizens of the world, we have various obligations to others. These are the moral and civil obligations we take on, and they can be divided into three main categories:

Public obligations. The most obvious public obligation we have is to pay our taxes and the like. If we are spiritual, we will look to the good of the country and pay them "freely and willingly, thinking it wrong to cheat and evade them" (TCR 430).

Domestic obligations. These are obligations that family members have to each other. These would include education of children, management of the home, and most of the other things that being part of a family entails (TCR 431).[1]

Private obligations. We incur many obligations in society: payment of wages to those who work for us, fulfilling contracts, paying interest on loans, and the like. We need to perform these obligations justly and faithfully (TCR 432).

The Lord is telling us to be decent human beings who fulfill their obligations and who don't take without giving. For instance, if you live in a country and benefit from its roads and laws and armed forces, you are obliged to support it.

Recreations of Charity

In addition to serving others in the form of jobs, benefactions, and duties, we need to renew ourselves so that we can serve again tomorrow. Though we may not normally think of it this way, recreation is actually an act of useful service, both because it allows us to serve others and because in rebuilding ourselves we share community and goodwill with those around us.

Recreation is useful and is an expression of charity because it diverts the mind from thinking about one's occupation and more importantly from the feelings involved in doing one's work. Each activity has its characteristic affection that "strains the mind and keeps it intent on its work or study. If it is not relaxed, it becomes dull and its desire flags" (Char 190). Diversion relaxes the mind; it is the proverbial unstringing of the bow (Ibid.). Too much focus on one thing drags us down. Engaging in a variety of activities, and with other people, brings new affections that can lift the depressive feelings that come with being over-focused (SE 3625). Recreation

---

[1] Some people take this on as their full-time job, in which case it is their primary occupation and belongs to the first category of uses we explored.

is about introducing our spirits to a variety of activities and so to a variety of emotional states, and these changes refresh us.

GIVING THE GIFT OF RECEIVING HELP

We normally think of serving as actively reaching out to others. Another way we serve is by willingly allowing others to serve us. Consider this important teaching: "Reward, for people who have charity, consists in their having the ability to do good, in being allowed to do it, and in the recipient's willing acceptance of it" (AC 3956). Many of us have had the experience of trying to help someone who clearly needed our help but who resisted it. By contrast, many have known the joy of having their proffered help gratefully accepted. That reception of aid is in itself a gift, our reward for the help we are trying to give.

Here's a personal story that drove this point home for me. When I was in college, my grandparents, then in their eighties, moved back to my hometown. I arranged for some friends to help me unload their moving van, which took an hour or two. The next day my grandfather gave me a very generous amount of money for each of the young men who had helped. I resisted, protesting that we had helped because we cared for him and he should let us help him. For perhaps the only time in my experience, he got annoyed with me, and said with some energy, "You had your fun. Now let me have mine!" My job was to graciously allow him to be kind to me.

CONCLUDING THOUGHTS

> *Heavenly joy ... is the pleasure of doing something which is of service to oneself or others. (TCR 734:)*

The Lord is calling us to become the kind of people who from our souls to our outmost beings long to serve others from love according to the Lord's wisdom. Our lower selves just know they want to be happy, and they believe that is our reason to exist. But we know that we are in this world to serve others, to make a difference to the people we come into contact with. In doing so, we open ourselves to the joy and peace the Lord yearns to give us. Knowing this and building our actions around this idea changes us. It takes us a lifetime, an eternity, in fact, to become what we would like to be, but it is a rewarding process, with each step forward giving us greater daily joy.

Perhaps the most surprising part of the Lord's teaching about doing good to others is that our primary way to make a difference in the world is through our daily work, not in the charitable actions we engage in outside of that work. This teaching calls us to embrace our jobs with a new spirit, to seek to bring a bit of heaven into our spirits and our workaday world. This approach allows our usefulness to blossom and bear fruit.

The three steps to becoming loving in this way are to turn to the Lord, shun evils that stand in the way, and then seek to do good to the best of our ability with all our heart.

ACTIVITIES AND QUESTIONS

1. What acts of service have made you feel most useful? When have you felt most happy? What did those experiences have in common? How were they different?

2. The Lord teaches that all heavenly happiness comes from being useful.
   a. What other things seem to be sources of happiness? What is the use in them? Do you need to reconsider these activities?
   b. What is one way of serving others that truly gives you joy? How many of them can you list?

3. Looking at your primary daily job or use, consider these questions:
   a. What do you find delightful or inspiring about your use?
   b. What spiritual qualities do you want to express in your use?
   c. What are challenges associated with your use?
   d. Who benefits because of your use? Let yourself think more broadly than just the obvious people.
   e. What is the biggest barrier you face to being useful? What might you do about that?

4. In what ways do you serve others as a good deed or benefaction?
   a. Do you have the proper balance of this kind of service in your life?
   b. Is there an area of need in the world or in your community that you feel called to serve more?

5. Are you fulfilling your public and private obligations? Are you doing so willingly and joyfully? If not, what stands in the way of doing this?

6. What do you do for recreation?
   a. Are there things you do to relax that in fact are simply avoidance techniques? What might you do instead that truly rejuvenates you?
   b. Do you think you have the proportion of work to recreation about right?

7. How does love for the Lord and for the neighbor show up in the various regular activities you engage in? To put it another way, how are others' lives better because you interacted with them in a loving way? Think about some simple things such as going to the grocery store, dealing with your mechanic, driving in traffic, or chatting with a neighbor with this question in mind.

Serve Others' Spiritual Needs: The Classes of the Neighbor

"Truly, I say to you, inasmuch as you did it to one of the least of these My brothers, you did it to Me." (Matt 25:40)

The last chapter focused on serving others as we commonly do in daily life. This chapter offers an opportunity to go deeper. The real purpose of spiritual living is to touch the spirits of those around us. While we are in this world, we cannot see another's spirit, so many of the ways we serve have to do with meeting external needs, and we end up guessing what would help them on a deeper level. As we know, this is a hit-or-miss proposition. We want to really help people but often do not know how.

The Lord has given a large body of teaching about the classes of the neighbor. These classes of the neighbor are described most generally in the parable of the sheep and the goats:

> Then the King will say to those on His right hand, "Come, you blessed of My Father, inherit the kingdom prepared for you from the foundation of the world: for I was hungry and you gave Me food to eat; I was thirsty and you gave Me drink; I was a sojourner and you took Me in; I was naked and you clothed Me; I was sick and you visited Me; I was in prison and you came to Me." Then the righteous will answer Him, saying, "Lord, when did we see You hungry and feed You, or thirsty and give You drink? When did we see You a sojourner and take You in, or naked and clothe You? Or when did we see You sick, or in prison, and come to You?" And the King will answer and say to them, "Truly, I say to you, inasmuch as you did it to one of the least of these My brothers, you did it to Me." (Matt 25:34-40)

The hungry, thirsty, sojourner, naked, sick, and imprisoned depict the six basic spiritual needs anyone can have, the six ways humans can be spiritually trapped, broken, or needy. An understanding of those needs offers us guidance about how to help people in each category (AC 2417:7-8, 3419:3-5). This way of understanding people was the wisdom of the ancients and was the basis for all their actions (AC 2417:7, 6705). In fact, the "whole doctrine of charity" is contained in the good we do to these six classes of the neighbor (HD 107). What follows is a brief sketch of a huge body of teaching that shows us some ways we can identify our neighbors' spiritual needs and give help more wisely. A more complete treatment can be found in *Exploring the Path*, 111-146.

Some people are uncomfortable with the idea of diagnosing the spiritual needs of others. Perhaps it is best to start with ourselves and those closest to us. As you

read, think about these two things: 1) *What are my needs right now?* As you become more familiar with your own needs, you come to know what to ask for and
also what to work on. As you become more comfortable with the classes of the
neighbor, you will feel more comfortable applying these ideas to others' situations.
2) *What do I think those closest to me need right now?* While you might be wrong,
you are showing love by trying to help those around you. This is what we do with
our loved ones all the time. When we do get it right, we will be able to help in ways
we never could have otherwise. This body of teaching is at the heart of becoming
a deeply loving person.

THE HUNGRY

> *I was hungry and you gave me food. (Matt 25:35)*
>
> *He satisfies the longing soul, and fills the hungry soul with goodness.
> (Ps 107:9)*

The spiritually hungry are "those who from affection desire good" (AC 4956,
2930:4). When we are hungry, we cry out to be filled, and those who are spiritually
hungry cry out to be filled with goodness of all kinds: a desire for spiritually loving,
compassionate hearts; a desire for the peace and satisfaction that comes from doing
the right thing; and an answer to loneliness, boredom, and fear. Their spirits might
be in danger of fainting away for lack of love in their lives. This desire is the most
basic human need.

Hunger, though it can be uncomfortable, is not a bad thing. If we did not become hungry, we would not want to eat and be filled. Because of this, Mary pro-
claims in the New Testament that the Lord "has filled the hungry with good things,
and the rich He has sent away empty" (Luke 1:53). When we are aware that we
need goodness, we become receptive to it; when we think we have all we need,
we don't seek more from the Lord or from others. "Blessed are those who hunger
and thirst for righteousness for they shall be filled" (Matt 5:6).

Do Good to People

> *To hunger is to eagerly desire what is good. (AC 4958)*

We feed the spiritually hungry when we do good to them (AE 287:11; AC 1458:2).
Sometimes doing good involves meeting a material or psychological need; at others
it involves meeting a spiritual need for goodness. We know how much a kind word
or thoughtful action means to us when we are sad or afraid. On the level of our

spirits, goodness is the ultimate reality; it is the food for our spirits that nourishes or satisfies (AE 750:10, 617:13). Think about how much even a sincere smile can help. Simply knowing that someone cares and seeks your good can be life changing. Consider what this world would be like if all of us treated each other with sincere kindness, with the genuine care that we offer in times of tragedy. Take that idea further and consider what the world would be like if we were genuinely interested in supporting and nurturing others' spiritual development and deepest spiritual needs.

Teach People about Goodness and Usefulness

A person shall not live by bread alone, but by every word that proceeds from the mouth of God. (Matt 4:3, 4; Luke 4:4; Deut 8:3)

Heavenly food in its essence is nothing else than love, wisdom, and useful service combined, that is, useful service accomplished through wisdom out of love. (ML 6:6)

Another way of feeding the hungry goes a step further, in keeping with the saying, "Give a person a fish, and you feed him for a day; teach him to fish, and you feed him for a lifetime." We offer more love and wisdom when we show spiritually hungry people how to bring goodness into their lives that they can then make their own (see AE 617:2–10, 146). We do this by offering truths that allow them to experience and express genuine goodness in keeping with the Golden Rule and the Two Great Commandments. Truths that lead people to understand and turn to the Lord bring goodness into their lives, as do truths about how to shun evils and so create space for the Lord's goodness. People who are spiritually hungry yearn particularly for truths that have direct application to their lives, truths that lead to goodness.

When we teach and encourage people to be useful, we are allowing the Lord to feed them. In many ways this is the governing idea about feeding people spiritually. Food means "everything that has a useful purpose" (AC 5293). Or as another teaching says, "Regarded in itself, good is nothing else than usefulness" (AC 4926). We see this illustrated in the rule that in the next life people receive food according to the use that they perform (AE 1194). Inviting someone to help us do something good for another person offers them food, and inviting them to nourish the spirit of another offers them food at a still deeper level.

Lead Them to Experience the Lord

In the end, feeding the hungry means leading people to the Lord. As He said, "The bread of God is He who comes down from heaven and gives life to the world.... I am the bread of life. He who comes to Me shall never hunger, and he who believes in Me shall never thirst" (John 6:33, 35). Because He is the bread of life, talking to someone about the Lord and His mercy and care might be offering food to the hungry in a more powerful way than offering helpful advice about how to solve their problems.

Another way to lead people to the Lord is by helping them to engage in the spiritual practices described in the second part of this book. Each spiritual practice causes us to stop for a time and give attention to the Lord rather than to life in front of us. Each time we do that, we open ourselves to His presence and goodness, which feeds us.

Symptoms of Spiritual Hunger[1]

- We yearn for affection, warmth, and consideration.
- We are deeply touched by acts of consideration shown to us.
- We want to make a difference.
- We want to help people in need.
- We want to make life better for people.
- We are ready to work. We are willing to serve.
- We feel passionate about what we're doing.
- We need opportunities to be useful.
- We feel limited in our ability to do what we want to do.

THE THIRSTY

> *I was thirsty and you gave me drink. (Matt 25:35)*
>
> *He who believes in Me shall never thirst. (John 6:35)*
>
> *"Behold, the days are coming," says Jehovah God, "That I will send a famine on the land, not a famine of bread, nor a thirst for water, but of hearing the words of Jehovah." (Amos 8:11)*

With the amazing teaching the New Church has been given, spiritual thirst is probably the easiest need to meet. The thirsty are those who "from affection desire truth"

---

[1] The lists of symptoms at the end of each class of the neighbor were originally developed by Rev. John Odhner. I have expanded on them.

(AC 4956; AC 8568:5), specifically truth from the Word or from genuine doctrine (AE 840:2; AR 50). We feed this need by giving people truths from the Word.

Spiritual thirst is similar to spiritual hunger in that people in both situations need to learn truth. But while spiritually hungry people want to learn truth that leads to doing what is good, spiritually thirsty people may be interested in truth for its own sake; if they see application, it might not be central to their desire (see AC 1460:2, 4, 1462:4). Their focus is on answers and understanding.

This search for truth has inherent dangers. The opposite of spiritual thirst is thirst for gaining truth from our own power or pride. This is not a humble seeking to receive truth from the Lord but is instead a fierce desire to uncover truth by our own intelligence. The Lord says that the truth we see to be from the Word is like a spring of water, while truth we derive from our own intelligence apart from the Lord is like broken, dirty cisterns carved out of rock (AE 483:8). Think, for example, about how much a proud person infuses false justifications into his position in order to deny being wrong.

Our journey of spiritual development involves coming to appreciate the pure water of life in ways we had not before. Spiritual struggles, or temptations, make us long for truth more intensely than at other times (AC 8568:10). In fact, one of the main results of temptations is to make us thirsty to imbibe truth more deeply than we had before (AC 6829). Just as bodily thirst leads us to seek out sources of liquid, so do times of spiritual struggle lead us to seek new truths because the truths we had feel inadequate. Spiritual struggles lead us to notice the dirt and contamination in the water we had been imbibing and to open ourselves more fully to the Lord's pure water of life.

Show People How to Find Truth for Themselves

Bringing water to the thirsty stands for giving instruction in truths to one desiring them, and so refreshing the life of their soul. (AC 8568:5)

Meeting the needs of the thirsty is simple. They want to be instructed in the truth (AC 8568:4-6, 2702:10). Because they tend to be motivated learners, our task is to help them make the truth their own (AE 617:2-3, 10). As well as teaching the truth directly, we can teach them to find the truth for themselves by taking them to the Word. Instead of giving them a fish, they want us to teach them how to fish. Or to put it another way, instead of teaching them truth, we can teach them to discover and understand it well enough that they can teach it to others. Inviting a spiritually thirsty person to join a study group with you is a good example of meeting that need. Inviting them to lead a study group might be even better.

Since we may be reluctant to "teach" our friends, perhaps a way of going about "giving instruction in truths" is to share our own understanding of what is true. We have an obligation to share what we know. In fact, that is one of the primary purposes of knowing truth:

> What is the use of knowing unless what is known to one be also known to others. Without this, what is knowing but collecting and storing up riches in a casket, and only looking at them occasionally, and counting them over without any thought of use from them? Spiritual avarice is nothing else. (ISB 18:2)

This sharing needs to be done with sensitivity to what people actually need, just as we would not help a naked person by giving them water or a hungry person by giving them medicine. But when we find spiritually thirsty people, the greatest gift we can give is to dive deeply into exploring the truth.

Symptoms of Spiritual Thirst

- We have questions. We want to learn.
- We want to help, but we don't know how.
- We love exploring and sharing new ideas.
- We are confused, don't understand, or have doubts.
- We feel challenged by other philosophies and ideas.
- We prefer to find things out for ourselves rather than having someone give us a quick answer.
- We think of ourselves as someone who has good ideas.
- We want to understand God, heaven, life, and love.
- We love digging deeply into the Lord's Word. We are inspired by the thought of spending a long period of quiet time reading.

THE SOJOURNER, OR IMMIGRANT[1]

> *I was a sojourner and you took Me in (Matt 25:35)*
>
> *I am a sojourner in the earth; do not hide Your commandments from me. (Ps 119:19)*

Spiritual sojourners are looking for community, for a new spiritual home. People who are entering a new community are changing their old patterns of living and adapting to new goodness and truth. All change means we are unsettled and vulnerable, and we need others to be sensitive to and aware of our needs, even more

---

[1]For this and the next three spiritual needs, I have drawn heavily from my book *Freely Give*, 148-79.

than they might be usually. Because of their search, sojourners are rootless and therefore need our support and protection.

At a more literal level, sojourners in the Old Testament were immigrants to Israel who wanted to adopt the Israelites' beliefs and customs. Because it is easy to see sojourners as different from ourselves, the Lord gave specific teaching about treating them with the compassion and respect we would want were we in their situation. The primary rule He gave was a version of the Golden Rule: "Also you shall not oppress a sojourner, for you know the heart of a sojourner, because you were sojourners in the land of Egypt" (Ex 23:9). He went even further by telling the Israelites to love sojourners as they loved their own (Lev 19:33-34; Deut 10:19).

The Israelites were supposed to leave the gleanings of the vineyard and the corners of their wheatfields for the poor and the sojourner (Lev 19:10, 23:22) or for the widows, orphans, and sojourners (Deut 24:19-22). In ancient times, before any social services existed, sojourners were vulnerable in the same way that a widow or an orphan was. Starvation and slavery were real possibilities.

We are all sojourners in the Lord's eyes (see Lev 25:23; Ps 39:12) because we are not born into heaven; instead, we are immigrants to heavenly life. We should treat others with the same sensitivity we would want directed toward us on our sometimes fumbling journey toward heaven and peace.

Show People the Basic Layout of the Land

> *Do not forget to entertain sojourners, for by so doing some have unwittingly entertained angels. (Hebrews 13:2)*

The key to discerning the needs of spiritual sojourners or immigrants is understanding their vulnerability. By thinking about the needs of someone traveling to a new land and culture, we can gain an idea of how to help them. They would not know the culture, the customs, the unwritten rules, or even where to go to find the basic necessities of life. They would long for a native of the land to offer "instruction" in how to get by and to fit in. That instruction would be practical—not a lecture on the history of the area's politics, but a description of the customs and practical realities. Similarly, a spiritual sojourner wants to be instructed about the truths of the church (AC 4956, 4444:5). Knowing the spiritual layout of the land makes them feel safe and that they belong.

The Lord says that we are supposed to "take in" (literally "gather in") sojourners. We would not offer help to sojourners at arm's length but rather would take them with us and show them around. We are not just teaching them; we are also offering them a community of support.

Sojourners want to belong, and our job is to help them do that. Those who are new to the church (or to a congregation, to marriage, to parenting, or to a job) are sojourners (AC 1463:2, 2049). They want to fit in and understand how to do things. Similarly, those who are new to a spiritual way of looking at themselves, dealing for the first time with their pride or temper or greed, are spiritual newcomers. They need acculturation, but just as much they need companions on their journey. Those companions will give them a sense of belonging.

Sojourners are courageous people, people who are willing to enter a new world and are willing and eager for others to tell them how to get along. If we can honor their courage and willingness to learn, we will be able to help them with a humility that respects their willingness to undertake a journey that we may never have had to take.

Symptoms of Being a Sojourner

- We want to connect with other people.
- We want to feel that we belong.
- We are lonely or need friendship.
- We want someone to listen.
- We want to be part of a community of people who share our values.
- We believe that nobody knows what we're going through.
- We feel lost and in need of direction.
- Our instinctual idea of the right path to follow often turns out to be incorrect.
- We don't feel at home in our culture and are looking for something better.
- We are looking for a new faith or church community.

THE NAKED

> *I was naked and you clothed Me. (Matt 25:36)*
>
> *He has clothed me with the garments of salvation, He has covered me with the robe of righteousness. (Is 61:10)*

Spiritually naked people are aware that they lack something they should have; they see that they lack goodness and truth in their lives (AC 4956) and as a result they are often doing what is wrong. Such people may experience worthlessness ("I'm no good") or confusion ("I don't understand at all"). They may experience grief or pain over loss of values or self-respect ("I thought I was an OK person, but I'm not"). Figuratively speaking, they are lacking beautiful clothing—thoughts that are positive, trusting, grateful, hopeful, confident, and that express the beauty and joy of life. Instead, they are naked, or partly so, wearing torn clothing or sackcloth or rags that symbolize negative thoughts, grief, shame, worthlessness, or loss. They may feel exposed and vulnerable. Natural clothing serves several functions: It gives us protection, warmth, comfort, privacy, and modesty, and it also expresses our identity. People who are experiencing loss, grief, shame, and worthlessness need truths that offer comfort, hope, affirmation of the Lord's love and goodness, and they also need acknowledgment of their own loss and lack in a setting that offers privacy, confidentiality, and safety.[1] Spiritually naked people see evil in themselves and lack the tools (truths) to do anything about it.

A specific and sadly common kind of nakedness comes from being stripped of truths by the actions of others. For instance, those who were abused as children may suffer this kind of nakedness. Because they were exposed to a harm they were in no way equipped to deal with, they were vulnerable, naked. One insidious effect of this harm is that people stay naked because they tend to imbibe falsities or lies that block out the healing power of the Lord's truth. ("It was my fault." "I am bad/tainted/beyond hope because of what happened to me." "Even the Lord could not love a person like me." "I have lost my hope of an eternal, happy marriage.") An even more insidious effect is that the shame of the abuse can lead people to act out in the very arenas in which they were harmed.

I used the example of abused children, but the same principle applies to people raised in a violent environment, those who were neglected as children, those who were raised with no clear spiritual guidance, and those who were taught false ideas that stripped them of the ability to grasp reality and thereby protect themselves from lies. These are a few examples of harm done to children that might cause spiritual nakedness. There are many kinds of harm done to adults that can cause them to be stripped naked spiritually.

States of Shame

When people are found naked, their natural reaction is one of shame. Spiritually naked people also seem easily susceptible to shame (see AC 213, 829). This shame will often cause in them a disproportionate sense of being wrong or bad. If you found someone who was naked, you would probably give that person clothing and then withdraw, allowing them to dress in private, without the embarrassment of being watched. Similarly, we help the spiritually naked by providing a strong sense of protection, honoring their dignity, and avoiding unintentionally causing more shame.

---

[1] This paragraph is slightly adapted from a passage in "Spiritual Care" by John Odhner (paper presented to the Council of the Clergy, 2017), 13; changed with permission.

Spiritually naked people often act out because of their shame, yet their behavior may not reflect what their inner self really wants to do or become. We would not stare at a naked person but would help them by giving them clothes. Similarly, we do well to pay less attention to the bad behavior of a spiritually naked person and more to calmly and without judgment helping them find a better way of acting.

Offer Tools and Truths

Because the naked lack truths (clothing) to cover their natural desires, it is not surprising that the Word seems to emphasize that we offer tools to naked people and let them use those tools as they see fit. After all, the naked are doing what is wrong by default, not with malicious intent. We have probably all known people who lived a wild and spiritually reckless life and then got married and settled down, apparently overnight, or the person who one day decided to get her life in order and within a few months was doing much better. The ability to change their lives so suddenly indicates that their evil actions were not deeply ingrained parts of their character. For such people, we offer insights and support as well as we can, and they will take the ideas that they find useful.

Symptoms of Spiritual Nakedness

- I feel low.
- I'm worried.
- I feel vulnerable.
- I'm struggling with grief.
- I'm struggling with shame.
- I don't want anyone to know what my issues are.
- I want to crawl in a hole and hide.
- I want to make peace with my past.
- I want something to look forward to.
- I'm no good. I have nothing to offer.
- I just don't want anyone to be hurt.
- I'm doing bad things reflexively and don't have the tools to stop.
- People I trust tell me that what I'm doing isn't good, but I don't yet see for myself that it's wrong.

THE SICK

I was sick and you visited Me. (Matt 25:36)

Heal me, O Jehovah, and I shall be healed; save me and I shall be saved, for You are my praise. (Jer 17:14)

Sick people are in a more spiritually dangerous position than the classes that have come before because they are doing evil that they know is wrong (AE 163:7; Jer 30:11-14; AC 8364). It could be a small sickness or a more advanced one, anything from taking office supplies from work or telling small lies to adultery or child abuse. All evil we do makes us spiritually sick; it is just a matter of degree. We might sometimes feel that we can help people who tell small lies but that someone who commits adultery and ruins a marriage is too far gone for us to help. But those involved in serious evil need our help most desperately. The world stands in deep need of a church and of individuals who are able to reach out with the healing truths of the Lord's Word, which are the healing truths of repentance. We can do this as fellow pilgrims on the journey toward spiritual health. Doing so with compassion makes a difference.

The Lord came on earth to heal the sick (Matt 9:10-13), and He calls us to reach out to them also. Yet evil is distasteful, and we may find that we want to distance ourselves from people who are doing what is wrong. Similarly, many diseases are unpleasant, and sick people can be challenging to be around. If we follow the Lord's example, we can help the sick by applying some of the principles that He used while on earth:

We have to get control of our own attitude first. When the Lord healed the sick, we are often told that He "had compassion" for them (Matt 14:14, 9:35-38). Can we have that same compassion when we deal with people who are sick? The Lord is the one who heals the spiritually sick, so to bring His presence we have to act toward those people from love.

We must also "visit" the sick. In all the prior spiritual needs, we are told to give people what they need: clothing for the naked, shelter for the sojourner, food for the hungry. But we are told to "visit" the sick. I believe this is because fundamentally the sick need to repent, and we cannot do that for them. But we can be present with them and "eat" with them, as the Lord ate with sinners and tax collectors (Matt 9:9-13).

It is useful to note that visiting does imply acknowledging that the person is ill. If you were to visit someone who was terminally ill and never show your awareness of their illness, that person would probably not feel comforted. Similarly, if we are to help spiritually sick people, we need to show that we are aware of their disorderly actions without dwelling on them. Otherwise our presence could be seen as condoning those disorderly actions.

On the other hand, I believe it is essential to express confidence that the person can overcome whatever evil is assailing him. We can say, in effect, "I believe that your best self doesn't really want this evil to be afflicting you. What can I do to help you address this threat to your spiritual life?"

We are told that "the sick are those who are distressed by evils and falsities, and are to be visited, by some who bring comfort and by others who bring a remedy" (SEm 4586). Sometimes we simply offer compassion; at other times we may be able to offer advice, direction, or words of support, particularly if we have struggled with that same evil ourselves.

We can encourage them to turn to the Lord, especially by repentance. Those who are sick have in some way turned their backs on the Lord. That's what spiritual sickness is: worshiping the gods of self-indulgent pleasure, power, pride, lust, or self-pity. The Old Testament repeatedly characterizes the Israelites' evil as turning away from Jehovah and worshiping other gods. The only way for the Israelites to be healed was to return to the Lord and ask for His help. The same is true for the sick.

Some things we could do to encourage repentance are talking about our journey in turning to the Lord, offering to accompany them to Holy Supper, praying with them, or talking about the teachings regarding the Lord's mercy and compassion and His power to help us when we are stuck. Only the Lord's love and power can heal, and sharing what we know about Him can be a tremendous gift. We will be most effective at doing this if we can reach out with the awareness that we, too, have been sick and easily could be again unless we turn to the Lord.

Symptoms of Spiritual Sickness

- I feel resentful or angry.
- I keep indulging unhealthy desires.
- I'm struggling with addiction.
- My life is falling apart.
- I have hurt people.
- People have hurt me.
- I'm sick of feeling pain.
- I feel controlled by anger, anxiety, greed, lust, pride, or the like.

The Imprisoned

I was in prison and you came to Me. (Matt 25:36)

If you abide in My word, you are My disciples indeed. And you shall know the truth, and the truth shall make you free. (John 8:31-32)

Since the spiritual needs get progressively more dire, it might be surprising to see the imprisoned listed after the sick. After all, what could be worse than intentionally doing what we know is wrong? The answer is: something that takes away our capacity to do what is right even if we want to. Prisoners, by definition, are not free. Whether they deserve it or not, they are forced to do certain things and are forbidden from doing others. In some cases, they suffer hardship and deprivation. Spiritual prisoners lack spiritual freedom because they are bound by the chains of falsity.

Another aspect of being in prison is missing out on real life. Imagine being a prisoner for twenty years, then going back to your old neighborhood. You would probably feel that it had changed enormously and, more important, that you had been left out of all the relationships that had developed while you were gone. You would lack the basic knowledge of what was right or wrong to do in many situations.

Spiritually imprisoned people are trapped by false ideas that compel them to act in evil ways. They cannot think straight because of the falsity, so their spiritual freedom is curtailed. The fundamental definition of spiritual prisoners is "those who acknowledge that there is nothing but falsity in themselves" (AC 4956; AC 8049). The effect of this false belief is that good and truth from the Lord cannot be perceived or lived (AE 724:17). The prisoner is trapped inside an artificial world created by the false belief.

Another kind of imprisonment is being in a state of denial, also known as self-justification. Inherent in falsity is the belief that the false way of viewing reality is true and therefore that reality is false (AC 5096). People who are naked or sick are also in prison when they deny that there is a problem. The path of redemption for them is to get out of prison first (acknowledge the truth of the situation), then work on getting spiritual clothing or medicine. Denial is probably at the heart of the most dangerous kinds of imprisonment because it prevents the trapped person from even seeing that there is a need to change.

In addition to destructive forms of imprisonment, good people become imprisoned during temptations because they become trapped by falsities (Rev 2:8-11; AE 122:1,5). The evil spirits with us bind the truths we know (AE 122, 138); then they bring forth the evils of our lives (AE 138). We are imprisoned because we feel that we cannot do what our inner self really wants to do (AC 7990).

Offer Our Perspective

Since the imprisoned are trapped by falsity they don't see, the most obvious service we can offer is to show them the falsity of their thinking (AE 724:17, 481:8). This is most often done by showing them truth that addresses the falsity. Meeting this need may require a more forceful statement of the truth than would be required to meet other spiritual needs because falsity is self-perpetuating; it offers false reasons why the truth is untrue. This means we may need to be direct and persistent with prisoners.

For those who are uncomfortable with the idea of instructing a friend, think of it as showing the friend reality. Someone in a troubled marriage may benefit from talking about relationships with someone in a functional marriage, not for a lecture, but for the subtle sharing that happens when we discuss with others. It might help the person see their own false ways of approaching their marriage. At times we may need to challenge false assumptions ("You cannot treat your wife that way if you expect her to stay with you"), but much of the time the person may learn from more gentle guidance.

Symptoms of Being Spiritually Imprisoned

- I feel stuck.
- I can't decide what direction my life should go.
- Something is wrong, and I don't even know what the problem is.
- I know my view of my life and of reality is inaccurate, but I don't know how to fix it.
- I have no control over my life.
- I can't make any progress.
- All my problems come from other people.
- Nothing I do makes any difference.
- I don't have any good options.
- I have made bad choices.
- I am engaging in a lot of escapist behaviors or thinking.

"You Did It to Me"

By this all will know that you are My disciples, if you have love for one another. (John 13:35)

If you love Me, keep My commandments. (John 14:15)

We would consider it a great day if we were able to truly help a fellow human being. Perhaps the most remarkable aspect of the parable the Lord told about the sheep and the goats in Matthew 25 is that by feeding the hungry, clothing the naked, and visiting the sick, we are also serving the Lord as if we'd done these things to Him. Anyone who is a parent understands this principle. If you do something kind to my child, it is as if you had done something kind to me, and perhaps even more so because I can take care of myself but my child cannot. Similarly, the Lord's love for us is so great that He sees our acts of service to each other as acts of love to Him. As the Lord says, the reason He considers acts done to others as acts done to Him is that He is in those who are spiritually hungry, thirsty, and the like because He is in anything good (AC 4959, 6711).

Concluding Thoughts

The Lord's teaching about serving the spiritual needs of others is a call to consider what we do in our daily lives more deeply than we naturally would. By taking the time to ponder and reflect on the needs of others, we offer them respect and love that will profoundly affect both the giver and the receiver. And in our reflection about their needs, and the humble questioning we'll inevitably do as we consider how to serve them, we will open our spirits to the Lord's guidance. In time, He will give us growing wisdom about how to serve others better.

As I said at the beginning, the first step is to try to identify our own spiritual needs and to ask for appropriate help. And our second step is to engage in helping those closest to us, respectfully and humbly. We are likely to find that seeking to serve others in this way will cause us to look more deeply and to build closer relationships with those around us.

The Lord's teaching about the classes of the neighbor shows us how to love others in the ways the Lord loves us. He offers us a chance to act as His agents—His angels—in touching the spiritual lives of those we come in contact with and to receive the joy that comes with serving the deepest needs of those we love.

ACTIVITIES AND QUESTIONS

1. What do you think your primary spiritual need is at this moment, recognizing that it might change?
   a. In the light of that primary need, what particular things do you need right now from the Lord and others?
   b. Does your primary need change if you think about your physical needs, then your emotional needs, and finally your spiritual needs?

2. In your best judgment, what would you say is the primary spiritual need of someone close to you?
   a. How might you treat that person differently based on that assessment?
   b. What new knowledge might you want to acquire about that person and about their spiritual need in order to serve them?

3. What would you say is the biggest spiritual need of your family or your community? How might you act differently based on this diagnosis?

PART 2
EXTERNAL SPIRITUAL PRACTICES

Without external worship we would have no knowledge at all of what is holy. (AC 1083:3)

We have been focusing on the essential elements of charity that are the core of spiritual practice. These internal practices allow the Lord to turn water into wine in us, symbolizing our transformation into spiritual, loving human beings (John 2:1-12). Yet as we have seen, external practices of charity are also necessary if we are to live as spiritual beings. They clothe and support the internal practices in a more profound way than is easy to see in our modern culture. We can think of the external practices as the vessels that contain our deeper transformation, so they are an integral part of the process of becoming more loving people. The rest of this book offers a guide to practical engagement in these external practices and can serve as a gateway to a conscious awareness of spiritual living and an intentional relationship with the Lord.

WHY THESE PRACTICES AND NOT OTHERS?

We live in a culture that values choices and dislikes being compelled to do specific things, especially doing them in a specific way. So why does the Lord ask us to emphasize these rituals and not others? It is not as if He didn't know about all the possible rituals that might exist. He chose these and offered a lot of teaching about them. It may be that we simply have to trust the Lord in giving us these particular practices.

These practices are also valuable because they give us the truths that support and contain the love we are supposed to express in our lives. Attending church and reading the Word expose us to the truths of the Lord's Word. Since we can learn to be loving only by means of the truths of the Word, these practices offer crucial help in our spiritual development. Nothing can take their place.

These external spiritual practices, as with any practices we engage in, make us exert discipline in our lives. We compel ourselves, and in that self-compulsion we assert our free will and humanity more than at any other time (AC 1937, 1947). That same discipline comes into play when we are facing our pride or greed or lust.

The primary reason for these practices, though, is that they turn us to the Lord as the source of love and direction. Each practice requires that we stop in our busy lives and give some attention to the Lord and to what He tells us is important. In the grand scheme, the Lord is not asking for that many of our 168 hours in a week. But He is asking us to acknowledge that He is the source of everything in our lives.

A Chance to Focus on the Lord

Do this in remembrance of Me. (Luke 22:19)

In our daily lives, we are faced with temptations to act in unloving ways, and we are given opportunities to act with love and compassion. So we look to the Lord, shun evils as sins, and serve others in our efforts to become more loving toward those around us.

We know that the Lord considers anything we do to someone else out of love as a kind deed done to Him (Matt 25:40). But that's different from consciously thinking about the Lord as we go through our daily life.

Paying attention to the Lord is important, and here we mean thinking about Him, talking to Him, reflecting on what He says in important, and the like. By way of example, imagine a person who is married and expresses his or her love by faithfully working hard to support the family, raising the children with integrity and kindness, doing chores around the house, and working diligently on his or her spiritual development so as to be a positive presence in the home, yet rarely interacts meaningfully with his or her spouse. They don't talk; they don't touch; they don't go on dates together; they don't consult about how to best manage a family and run a household together. Clearly something vital would be missing.

Similarly, much of spiritual living leads us to turn to the Lord indirectly. We turn to Him for help in shunning evils or for the power to act with love. In these times our focus is on the people in front of us or on our own lives, just as the married partner in the illustration above was focused on the task at hand. When we take up the external spiritual practices the Lord tells us to, our focus changes. Each of them leads us to give conscious attention to the Lord directly:

- When we pray, we enter into conversation with the Lord.
- When we read the Word, we learn what the Lord has to say about many things.
- When we attend church, we thank the Lord and ask for His influence in our life, both in our hearts and in our minds.
- When we take Holy Supper, we acknowledge that we do not have the strength to carry on without Him.
- When we reflect on our lives in the light of the Word, we offer the greatest compliment of being willing to pattern our lives on what He teaches.

- In all these things, we stop; we put our lives on hold for a while, acknowledging that the Lord is worth our time and attention.

If we think of each of these practices as a way to see and connect with the Lord, we realize that they could make our relationship with the Lord come alive with a sense of purpose and intimacy. In the example of a human marriage, the time spent face to face talking and enjoying activities together would make all the other things the couple was doing so much more effective because of the sense of connection and support. Each of these external spiritual practices makes the Lord a companion and guide in our daily life in a much more conscious way than He could be otherwise. They enable us to have a relationship with Him.

CAN WE DO TOO MUCH OF A GOOD THING?

Although the Lord is very clear that we need to engage in external spiritual practices, He also wants us to see that these practices support and inform the internal spiritual practices of turning to Him, repenting, and serving others. Throughout history, people have believed that a life of piety (prayers, reading the Word and other spiritual books, meditation on spiritual matters) was real spiritual living, that they should devote as much of their attention to these matters as possible, and that living in a convent or monastery was more spiritual than daily interaction in a life in the world. It turns out that this is an illusion, an attempt to live in the spirit apart from the body (HH 528). As we have seen, true spiritual living involves the inner practices of turning to the Lord, shunning evil, and serving others, not sequestering ourselves from everyday living.

People who focus too much on a life of piety, especially when they do this instead of living an active life of service to others, develop a "sorrowful life that is not receptive of heavenly joy" (HH 528). They think they are earning heaven by these actions, but they are actually thinking of themselves and the good things they have earned as they do these actions. This self-absorption makes them unreceptive of heavenly joy (HH 535).

So can we do too much of a good thing? Yes, if we spend time on spiritual practices at the expense of living a good life. But if we use the practices to enhance our relationship with the Lord and to learn to be a better person, then these practices will be time well spent.

Attend Worship

Surely you shall keep My Sabbaths, for it is a sign between Me and you throughout your generations, that you may know that I am Jehovah who sanctifies you. You shall keep the Sabbath, therefore, for it is holy to you. (Ex 31:13, 14)

Anyone in whom ... charity is present keeps the Sabbath holy since nothing is sweeter than worshiping the Lord and declaring His glory day by day. (AC 1798:2)

For many of us, it's not obvious what we gain from going to church. Perhaps we have experienced times when worship felt enjoyable in a spontaneous way, such as a service around Christmas when everyone was in a good mood, and we were able to get caught up in the idea of the Lord's being born in our hearts. Unfortunately, worship does not always feel that way, and instead we can feel that it is a burden or an unpleasant duty. Then the temptation is to find reasons not to go to church or to see going to church as a duty rather than a joy.

I once heard a story that someone who had to attend worship twice a day during high school years calculated that he had banked enough worships to get off attending any more Sundays until he was 83! Obviously we can't bank worship any more than we can gorge ourselves once a month and then avoid eating for the rest of the month. The point of worship is that it is more like eating—a necessary and important event that we wouldn't want to miss.

People who work hard often feel that Sunday is their only day to relax, which we know is both spiritually and psychologically important. Since attending church can feel like a chore, we might be tempted to put it off just as we might household chores. Unlike housecleaning or other tasks that we can postpone and then catch up on later, we won't be spurred to get to church by any external sign that we need it. Plus the benefits accrue quietly and slowly because they are deep ones.

Probably the main reason we are tempted to avoid church is that we feel we don't get enough out of it to warrant the effort. I hope you will see from this chapter that the benefits of worship are often deeper and more powerful than we readily see or feel. What we give our time and attention to defines our values as nothing else can, so the choice to attend church says that the Lord is important to us.

In fact, worship is less about getting something than about giving something back to the Lord. Stopping to give the Lord our time and attention opens our hearts and spirits in a way that nothing else can and initiates deep changes in our lives.

As we will see, the Lord is quite clear that attending church is important and valuable. I invite you to consider ways you can see His loving, compassionate invitation to embrace attending church as a valuable, important, and ultimately stress-relieving activity.

THE BENEFITS OF WORSHIP

When we go to church, we want to be inspired, and this is a worthy goal. Ideally, we would be inspired all the time, but sometimes we are not. Yet the Lord is clear that we receive important benefits, many of which are too deep and powerful for us to notice at the time. So let's review some of the things we gain through worship.

We saw earlier that worship has a lot to offer: Spiritual practices call to mind deeper spiritual qualities that ordinary living does not; we humble ourselves in worship, which allows the Lord to be present with us in ways He could not be otherwise; the Lord creates order in our lives by means of worship; intentional external worship can lead to being joined to the Lord; the benefits to our spirits are far greater than we can be consciously aware of; because we invite the Lord in by means of worship, He can protect us; and our external actions in worship create a vessel for the internal qualities we are developing by looking to the Lord, shunning evils, and doing what is good (p. 7). We could also list other benefits, such as experiencing community when we worship together; learning new things about how to be a spiritual person; being uplifted by inspirational music, by the Word, and by preaching; and the like.

Modern culture has moved away from ritual observance and often avoids the commandment to remember the Sabbath. This started when the Lord came on earth and observance of Jewish law ended, including the prohibition of working on the Sabbath. Worship attendance was essential for salvation for Catholics because they believed unconfessed sins were spiritually fatal. While still important for Protestants, worship attendance was less central to spiritual living. In recent years, ritualistic behavior has become even less important to many and is often considered to be irrelevant. We'll explore why attending church is important, as well as how to go about getting the most out of our worship experiences.

REMEMBER THE SABBATH DAY TO KEEP IT HOLY

Six days you shall work, but on the seventh day you shall rest; in plowing time and in harvest you shall rest. (Ex 34:21)

When the Lord gave us the ten basic laws of spiritual living, one law involved taking a day off to worship Him: "Remember the Sabbath day to keep it holy." In fact, "the Sabbath was the holiest thing among the children of Israel because it represented the Lord" (TCR 301). For the Israelites, the holiness of the Sabbath lay in taking time out for the Lord, even during the busiest times of plowing and harvest, to recognize that His salvation was more important than anything.

Applying this commandment today can seem like a sticky issue because we're so busy. Can we really afford to take a day off from life? If we do so, we want to know what we're getting in return.

One answer is that the Sabbath is not about what we receive but about what we give. We are acknowledging that the Lord is important enough to warrant some of our time. This is similar to everyday life in that we do many things purely for others. We drive slower as we pass a pedestrian so that the pedestrian is not nervous; we greet guests as they enter our house so they feel welcome; we smile and wait for someone who is moving slowly through the checkout line even though we are in a rush. The commandment about the Sabbath is partly about doing something for someone else. We stop to say, "The Lord is important enough that I am willing to change my life patterns to honor Him and to give over a day to worship, reflection, and actions that He considers most important" (see AC 9449). The Lord's wish for us on the Sabbath is clear in this teaching:

> If you turn back your foot from the Sabbath, from doing your will on My holy day, and call the Sabbath an honorable delight to the Holy One of Jehovah; if you honor it, not going your own way, or seeking your own will, or speaking a word; then you shall take delight in Jehovah, and I will make you ride on the high places of the earth; I will make you eat with the heritage of Jacob your father, for the mouth of Jehovah has spoken. (Is 58:13-14)

At root, the Sabbath is about doing what is pleasing to the Lord rather than seeking our own pleasure, and in time we will find delight in doing so. This is similar to the way a marriage involves coming to find delight in doing what makes the other person happy. We certainly should be trying to do what is pleasing to the Lord every day, but the Sabbath is perhaps a time to be consciously thinking of would delight Him.

Let's dig a bit more into this commandment. What does it mean to "remember" the Sabbath to keep it "holy"? We remember things that ordinarily we would forget.

Remembering the Sabbath is about paying attention to the Lord and His way of doing things in a way that we don't normally do, including the ways we remember Him during the week. Since the Lord is the only person who is holy, we make the Sabbath holy by inviting Him into it. Just as He asked of the Israelites, the Lord asks us to stop for Him, to remember Him for a time each week.

The Lord gives us specific instruction about what remembering the Sabbath means for us today: "When the Lord came into the world ... the Sabbath day was turned into a day for instruction in divine things, for rest from labors, for meditating on things related to salvation and eternal life, and for loving our neighbor" (TCR 301; AE 54). The passage goes on to emphasize two of these—instruction and loving our neighbor—as the main focuses for us today.

The inner meaning of the commandment supports the idea of stopping. The command to avoid doing any work means that we are not to do anything that begins in ourselves but "what begins in the Lord" (AC 8495:3-4). So on the Sabbath we are to give special attention to activities that come from the Lord and that remind us of Him, and we are to put aside things that distract us from Him and His values. This is similar to the way all relationships need time when we put aside all other activities and give the other person our full attention.

We can gain insight into the Sabbath by understanding that it literally means "rest" and has the connotation of "peace" (AC 10730:2; HH 287:2; TCR 303). In fact, "the Sabbath consists in rest"[1] (AC 10369:6). The Sabbath is a time for putting away our struggles and seeking peace. While we can be at peace during any activity, we experience peace far more easily when our minds are unoccupied by things that cause anxiety. Resting (stopping what we could be doing) and turning to the Lord allows us to experience Him (see AC 8455). Stopping because we are making the Lord a priority forces us to confront our anxieties that suggest that our work, not the Lord's presence in our lives, is what makes us successful.

One more teaching shows us the importance of the Sabbath: Even in heaven the angels have worship services that are their "Sabbath" (ML 23; see also ML 9:4). Stopping to give time and attention to the Lord, then, is not just an external event useful for children. It is something we need as children and continue to need for all eternity.

How can we put the Sabbath back in Sunday? Seeing the Sabbath as important is the first step. It is a time for stopping and acknowledging the Lord and of seeking peace, reflection, and instruction.

---

[1] As this passage shows, much of this rest is internal—the spiritual peace and rest that come when we conjoin goodness to truth in our lives. It seems clear from this and many other teachings that getting to this point requires a time of rest from worldly concerns.

ESSENTIAL ELEMENTS OF WORSHIP

Love worships; what is loved is worshiped. (AC 10414)

The purpose of all worship is communication with heaven, and through this the Lord's being joined to people. (AC 10436e)

Perhaps we can agree that we want peace and we want to focus on the Lord for our Sabbath. We may then ask, does church need to be a certain way or look a certain way if we are to obtain the benefits of worship? The bigger question is, do we have to be in a certain state of mind to benefit from worship?

There are some indications that the form of worship people commonly use, such as hymns, prayers, readings, and a sermon, is pretty good. We are told that worship in heaven is quite similar in its external form to worship on earth (HH 221). This suggests that what we think of as the normal church experience is spiritually valuable.

Rather than focusing on forms of worship, the Lord emphasizes the key qualities we should bring to and look for in worship because they are what make our worship genuine. They challenge us a little because they are not a simple list of external things, such as what we should wear. Instead, they are qualities of true worship that can exist within many external forms of ritual.

While many of these elements of worship could be used to design a worship service, I would encourage you to turn it around: Try to bring each of these qualities with you to worship, whatever your service may look like. If you do, you're likely to find that you will get much more out of any worship service you attend.

These are the core principles of worship:

- The Lord must be the center of all worship.
- Worship must be based on principles drawn from the Word.
- Worship needs to be an extension of our life.
- Worship involves humility and submission of our will to the Lord's.
- Worship needs to involve adoration of the Lord.

We are also told that worship requires innocence, that it should be reverent, and that it should be joyful, though these qualities are not emphasized nearly as much as those listed above. (For more see *Exploring the Path*, 164-173.)

We can see that these qualities could exist in a wide variety of settings and services. Different cultures will look at these principles of worship and apply them in many ways. Some cultures might apply the concept of praising the Lord by dancing (Ps 149:3, 150:4) or by clapping hands (Psalm 47:1). Others might bow with their faces to the ground instead of kneeling (AC 1999). It is useful to acknowledge that there is a basis in the Word for a wide variety of forms of worship, sometimes even among people in the same congregation. Our job is to choose something that reflects those principles the best we can for our particular culture and setting.

One of the invitations to worship we sometimes hear is, "Jehovah is in His holy temple. Let all the earth keep silence before Him" (Hab 2:20). Worship creates a space within which we can turn to the Lord and experience Him.

What We Bring to the Service Matters Most

What we bring to a worship service is far more important than what happens there. When we go to see a show, we expect to be entertained. It is the job of the performer to make us feel good. But church is not entertainment; it is worship. In worship we are active participants, and what we think and feel matter more.

Consider a few attitudes that reflect the principles of worship we explored just above. We make the Lord the center of our worship when we go to church saying, "The Lord is so important that He is worth this hour of my time each week." We make the Word important in our worship when we arrive with the awareness that the Word holds many pearls of wisdom and application that we don't know. When we show up at church looking for life application, we are more likely to find it. When we hold in mind what the Lord has done for us in the last week, we are able to adore and thank Him freely and from the heart. If we can reflect on areas of our lives that are not working as well as we would like, we can come to church with a spirit that is open and willing to be touched—a humble spirit. In each example, what we get out of the service is more about the attitude and approach we bring to the service than about anything that happens there.

Holding these attitudes will not magically change everything. A particular service may be a poor fit for what we seek. A minister may be ineffective or a mismatch for our needs. We may be in an agitated state of mind or going through something that prevents us from feeling any benefit. But that is similar to anything we do. Not every service will be a perfect fit, but if we can approach worship knowing that what we bring to the service is the most important thing, we will likely find the service to be much more satisfying.

WHAT TO DO ON THE SABBATH

We know we should go to church on Sundays, but what else? The Lord tells us about a number of things we could focus on during our Sabbath that would help us in our lives.

On the Sabbath we are to *make time for instruction in divine things and in matters of life* (TCR 301; AC 10360:8; AE 54, 537:6; see also Mark 6:2). It is notable that in the Heavenly Doctrines, the Lord focuses far more on instruction in a worship service than on the humility and praise that come in the prayer and singing portions. He certainly values the other parts of worship, but the focus is on learning. This suggests that in addition to going to church, it would be a good idea to spend time on Sundays reading the Word. As we'll see when we explore the practice of reading the Word, our Sunday reading should be for the sake of applying what we learn to our lives rather than for intellectual understanding.

The Sabbath is also a time for *rest from labors* (TCR 301). This means not getting too caught up in busywork, and it specifically means not doing the kind of work we do during the week.[1] This is a day for spiritual rejuvenation. The story of Mary and Martha is relevant here. The Lord had come to visit, and Martha was "distracted with much serving" while Mary sat at the Lord's feet to listen to Him. When Martha complained about Mary's not helping, the Lord supported Mary, telling Martha that she was "worried and troubled about many things" while Mary had chosen "that good part, which will not be taken away from her." (Luke 10:38-42). The Sabbath is a time for putting aside worries, not thinking about how to pay the bills or what to do with that problem at work, and instead focusing on the good things the Lord's presence brings. It takes discipline to stop dealing with our daily concerns, particularly in this electronic age when our work follows us home, and social media sends out a barrage of messages that seem important and even urgent. We need to say no to these things in order to say yes to the peace the Lord is offering us.

The Sabbath is also a time to *meditate on matters relating to salvation and eternal life* (TCR 301) and *about the Lord* (AC 10356). This means that we need to spend time reflecting on our own lives and how they are going. It might be useful on Sundays to take an inventory of how the week went, spiritually speaking. What went well? What would be useful to give particular attention to in the upcoming week? It would also be useful to think about the Lord and His care for us.

Finally, on the Sabbath we are to *love our neighbor* (TCR 301; see also Matt 12:10-13; John 5:1-16). We might ask how we are supposed to love the neighbor on the Sabbath in a way that is different from what we do on the other days. One possible answer is that we could engage in charitable actions that are different from our day-job: We can do good deeds to the needy, fulfill the duties of charity, and engage in the recreations of charity. We can serve others and socialize with them

---

[1] Some people work on Sundays, such as ministers, providers of essential services (medical personnel, police, etc.), and caregivers. In such a situation, a person would have to find some other time to stop and make the Lord a priority.

as a way to show love for them while at the same time giving us a break from our daily work so we can return to it refreshed.

CLEAR PRINCIPLE, FLEXIBLE APPLICATION

> *The Sabbath was made for man, and not man for the Sabbath. Therefore the Son of Man is also Lord of the Sabbath. (Mark 2:27-28)*

The Lord made this statement after He had healed on the Sabbath, seemingly breaking Sabbath laws about doing no work. In fact, in the eyes of the Pharisees, the Lord repeatedly broke both the actual Old Testament laws and the Pharisaic tradition by healing, plucking grain, and the like. His answer to these accusations was that Sabbath law was not designed to control people but to serve them: The Sabbath was made for man and not man for the Sabbath. This means that the teaching about remembering the Sabbath is adaptable. Yes, we should remember the Sabbath, but we may observe our Sabbath on Saturday if we work on Sunday. Or we may have an hour of Sabbath time every day that is a powerful time of stopping. Unlike the rest of the Ten Commandments, the Lord tells us directly that there is flexibility in our application of the external aspects of this law.

CLOSING THOUGHTS

Setting aside time each week to honor and worship the Lord can feel like lost time because we are not doing what ordinarily captures our attention or feels useful. Yet, as in any relationship, we show that we value someone by giving them our time and attention. It is not unreasonable to expect to set aside time each day and each week for the Lord, to build our relationship with Him.

The time that we offer to the Lord is a tool He uses to open us to Him so He can fill our spirits with goodness. We open our spirits to the Prince of Peace when we stop to pray, when we take time out from worldly concerns to focus on spiritual living, and when we arrange our lives to make going to church a deep value that we prioritize over other activities. We may lose what we think of as free time by doing this, but what we gain is the Lord's presence, a growing sense of connection with Him, and the peace and hope His presence brings.

ACTIVITIES AND QUESTIONS

1. What inspires you to attend worship?

2. What are the main barriers that keep you from attending worship or from engaging fully in worship when you do attend?

3. Which of the principles of worship could you most usefully focus on more during your worship experiences?

4. Worship is supposed to help us come to know and love the Lord and our neighbor better. What could you do to hold this intention more clearly in mind when you go to church?

5. What would your life look like if your Sunday were focused on the activities described in this chapter?

6. How does your Sabbath practice show up in everyday living?

Participate in the Holy Supper

The Holy Supper was instituted by the Lord to be a means of joining the church with heaven, and so with the Lord. That is why it is the holiest part of worship. (HD 210)

The Holy Supper is an external practice of the church that has an internal reality within it, and by means of this reality it joins one who is governed by love and charity to heaven, and by means of heaven to the Lord. (AC 4211)

For many, Holy Supper is the most challenging ritual of worship to engage in because it is unclear why the act of eating unleavened bread and drinking wine makes a meaningful difference to our lives. In recent years, attendance at Holy Supper has diminished even more than attendance at worship.

The Lord tells us that Holy Supper is the "means of joining the church with heaven, and so with the Lord" (HD 210; TCR 621:13). That is a remarkable statement, particularly since joining heaven with the church in us is our reason for being on earth. We know that the more common teaching is that true worship is not engagement in ritual but instead involves living according to what the Lord teaches (AC 10143:3-6, 8252-57, 7038). How, then, are HD 210 and similar passages also true? What does the ritual of Holy Supper add or change? How does it introduce us to heaven in a way that ordinary spiritual living does not? We will explore these questions over the course of this chapter and discover how a deeper understanding of how Holy Supper works can lead us on the path to experiencing heaven right now.

CORRESPONDENCES ARE THE KEY

"The person who eats My flesh and drinks My blood abides in Me, and I in him." (John 6:56)

The idea of eating the Lord's flesh and drinking His blood is startling, even repulsive. However, New Church teaching is clear that we are not to take this literally. These are symbolic acts. The Lord's flesh (the bread) symbolizes His Divine goodness, and His blood (the wine) symbolizes His Divine truth (TCR 711). As external as eating bread and drinking wine are, the true value comes from being aware of the deeper things we are also taking in. Holy Supper offers a complete connection with the Lord, from the inmost to outmost parts of us.

In Holy Supper we come humbly before the Lord, acknowledging that on our own we do not have the power to conquer our evils or to do what is good. We take in the bread and wine as a symbol of asking the Lord for His love and wisdom in our spirits. And by doing something with our bodies that mirrors what we are seeking to do with our spirits, we create vessels within ourselves that allow the Lord to work a powerful change.

By way of analogy, think about the power of touching someone you love. Imagine a loved one in the hospital and susceptible to infection. You can see her and talk to her but only through a glass partition. What a difference it would make to be next to her, holding her hand, embracing her. Holy Supper is an opportunity to touch and be touched by the Lord in a unique way. It offers us a heart-connection that has special impact, and it is grounded in a physical experience that makes that inner connection more lasting and more immediately powerful.

That said, we all know that there is no inherent holiness in the external elements by themselves. They are simply containers for the deeper idea of the Lord's love and wisdom that we hope to receive (AR 224:13). To return to our analogy, touching the hand of that loved one is not the goal; it is the means to connecting with her spirit.

HOLY SUPPER AS A SACRAMENT OF REPENTANCE

Although not its only use, Holy Supper serves as a means of helping us in our work of repentance. We are told to go through the steps of repentance "once or twice a year when you go to Holy Communion" (AR 531:5), and to be successful in doing that, we need help. By ourselves, we are not capable of resisting evil. The Lord resists for us when we make an effort as if by ourselves (AC 3927:2). When we turn to the Lord in Holy Supper, we acknowledge our need for Him in our effort to repent, and He strengthens us in it.

Although there is a connection between Holy Supper and repentance, we can still take Holy Supper if we have not recently gone through a process of repentance. The teaching seems to be that we must have a general pattern of repenting from evils, and when doing so we can use Holy Supper as an aid. However, we should not attend Holy Supper if we are involved in evil that we have no intention of refraining from.

HOLY SUPPER IS ABOUT HOW WE LIVE

In *True Christian Religion*, the Lord spends a lot of time describing what it means to attend Holy Supper worthily and unworthily. The basic teaching is that those who are regenerate can take Holy Supper worthily because they have faith in the Lord and charity toward the neighbor (TCR 722-24). Because of this teaching, some people have shied away from taking Holy Supper for fear that they are unworthy. Few of us would confidently assert that we have been regenerated!

The context for the Lord's teaching about worthiness is the Catholic tradition of taking Holy Supper at every worship service; this could lead to doing it as a matter of routine rather than intentionally. The Lord wants us to avoid mindless engagement in a spiritual ritual, especially when we do not intend to change our life (AE 250:4). True unworthiness comes from being set on evil, expressed in one passage as "contempt for the Lord and for the good and truth of faith, and hatred toward the neighbor" (AC 3601:2). Instead, the teaching that we need charity in our lives means that we need to approach Holy Supper with the "full purpose of amendment of life" rather than being involved in evil without any attempt to change (TCR 722:2-3). Approaching Holy Supper worthily is not about being perfect or having completed our spiritual work but is instead about having an inward desire to turn to the Lord and to follow Him in spite of our imperfection (TCR 723). In short, if we are trying to turn to the Lord to change our lives, we are approaching the Holy Supper worthily.

WHY WE SHOULD TAKE THE HOLY SUPPER

We have seen that taking the bread and wine of Holy Supper symbolizes taking in the Lord's love and wisdom. If we do this with a desire to change our lives, then we take Holy Supper worthily. But this does not explain why it is so important to take Holy Supper. Here are a few teachings about this. I explore them in more detail in *Exploring the Path*, 182-188.

The main reason to take Holy Supper is that *the Lord commanded it:* "Do this in remembrance of me" (Luke 22:19). Another reason is that *its holiness changes us.* We hear the term "Holy Supper" so often that we may pass over what it means for something to be holy. It means that the Lord, who is the source of holiness, is present in a special way, and His holy presence changes us. Because it changes us, *the angels see us differently.*

A teaching that is important but less immediately clear is that *we approach the Lord in a unique way:* "The Lord is wholly present in the Holy Supper, and so is the whole of redemption" (TCR 716). There appears to be something special about His presence during Holy Supper (AC 4211, 4217). "In order that everyone ready to repent *might look to the Lord alone*, the Lord instituted the Holy Supper, which confirms the remission of sins in people who repent. It confirms this, because in that Supper or Communion everyone is kept looking to the Lord alone" (DP 122).

Though not obvious to us, Holy Supper is designed to keep us focused on the Lord Jesus Christ as the one God in ways we would not normally be.

Another reason to take Holy Supper is that *it introduces us into a new spiritual state in a ritual way*. The Lord tells us that Holy Supper offers a different *kind* of help than normal living does: It is a formal way of connecting to and committing to spiritual living. In one teaching the Lord says that Holy Supper is a "sign and seal" of the joining together with the Lord that comes through spiritual living (AC 10522). In another passage the Lord calls it "an assurance and a certification" that those who live well will be saved (AE 1180e). And we are told that "Holy Supper is a guarantee and seal put upon the adoption as children of God of those who approach it worthily" (TCR 728). Similar to a wedding ceremony or an induction ceremony for a judge or military officer, Holy Supper brings us into a new state that our inner work has readied us for (see TCR 721).

THE LORD *WANTS* THIS CONNECTION WITH US

> *"With fervent desire I have desired to eat this Passover with you before I suffer." (Luke 22:14)*

When the Lord introduced the Holy Supper to His disciples, He was about to undergo the most severe temptation of His time on earth. This event was the last significant interaction He had with His disciples before His resurrection. We could think of His words as we might think of our own final words on earth to a loved one. In that last time, He reached out: "With fervent desire I have desired to eat this Passover with you." And then He introduced the Holy Supper. Perhaps more than anything, we need to know that the Lord is earnestly inviting us to come to the Holy Supper.

ACTIVITIES AND QUESTIONS

1. How important is Holy Supper in your life? What could you do to make it more meaningful?

2. What, if any, obstacles do you experience at the thought of taking Holy Supper?

3. Why do you think the Lord chose bread and wine as the elements of His supper rather than many other things that could have represented His love and wisdom?

4. What other rituals in your life connect you to the Lord?

Pray to the Lord

I love Jehovah, because He has heard My voice and my supplications. Because He has inclined His ear to me, therefore I will call upon Him as long as I live. I will take up the cup of salvation, and call upon the name of Jehovah. I will pay my vows to Jehovah now in the presence of all His people. (Ps 116:1, 2, 13, 14)

Prayer is probably the most common external spiritual practice, which is good because the Lord says we are to "set aside plenty of time" for it (AC 8253). It is the simplest to do, and we can do it in the midst of a busy meeting or a traffic jam. It can bring the most obvious immediate results, yet it is also the most ephemeral and unmeasurable of the spiritual practices. If you go to church, you know you've done something. If you read the Word, you have learned or been reminded of something. If you reflect on your life, you gain clarity. What exactly does prayer accomplish and how?

When many people in the New Church talk about prayer, they refer to the following passage, which covers many of the principles of prayer in one short paragraph:

Prayer, regarded in itself, is speech with God, and at the same time some inner view of the things being prayed for. Answering this there is something like an influx into the perception or thought of the mind, so that there is a certain opening of the person's interiors toward God. But the experience differs according to the person's state, and according to the essence of the subject of the prayer. If a person prays from love and faith, and for only heavenly and spiritual things, there then comes forth in the prayer something like a revelation, which is manifested in the affection of the one who prays as hope, consolation, or a certain inward joy. It is from this that to "pray" symbolizes in the internal sense to be revealed. (AC 2535)

We'll go through elements of this teaching in this chapter. In essence, we could say that prayer is talking to the Lord and receiving an answer. That answer will vary depending on our state and on the nature of our prayer.

THE BASICS OF PRAYER

When we think about prayer, what are the foundational teachings in Scripture and in the Heavenly Doctrines that should guide our thinking? One story in Scripture encapsulates many important aspects of prayer. A man had a demon-possessed son and brought him to the disciples, but they could not heal him. When the Lord arrived, He said to the man, "'If you can believe, all things are possible to one who believes.' Immediately the father of the child cried out and said with tears, 'Lord, I believe; help my unbelief!'" The Lord then healed his son (Mark 9:14-29). There are many dynamics at play in this story. Why couldn't the disciples heal the boy? What was it about the man's touching confession (prayer) that allowed the Lord to heal his son? We'll explore possible answers as we examine some of the essential elements of prayer.

Look to the Lord: "Prayer Is Talking with God"

In the story, the man's son is healed, not when he speaks to the disciples, but when he speaks directly to the Lord. Prayer is talking with God, not with someone else. And it is talking *with* God, not talking *at* God. Probably all of us have found that at times we are not really talking with the Lord but rather are just sounding off. There are times when we need somebody to listen to us, but we don't really care who it is. While it's good that we choose to pray at such times, we're not actually talking with the Lord so much as venting.

For Christians, praying means looking not just to God in broad terms, but to the Lord:

> Today a new angelic heaven is being ... made up of those who believe in the Lord God the Savior and who go directly to Him.... From now on all people from Christian areas who do not believe in the Lord are not going to be listened to, either. (TCR 108)

This shift from looking to God to looking to the Lord is depicted in our story. The man first took his son to the disciples, but they could not heal him. The disciples represent the doctrine or teaching of the church—its truths and ideas. We cannot be healed by ideas, or by an invisible God. We are healed by the Lord Jesus Christ, a visible, personal, yet infinite God who loves us.

Intend to Change Your Life

To be effective, prayer needs to be an extension of the way we are living. The man who brought his son to be healed was willing to change himself so that his son could be healed. The Lord teaches that "worship does not consist in prayers and in external devotion, but in a life of charity. Prayers are only its externals because they come out of a person by his or her mouth. Therefore a person's prayers have the same quality as the person's life" (AE 325:3).

Sometimes we pray for things that are completely beyond our control—for the well-being of a loved one, for the Lord to show us our eternal partner, for the spread of the church, or for peace in a war-torn part of the globe. We make such a prayer genuine, I believe, if we would do something to bring it about if we could. In that sense, prayer is not just something we say but something we intend.

The man with the demon-possessed son was clearly living what he professed. He said, "Lord, I believe," meaning that he was walking the path of belief. And then he asked for help. We know that the Lord healed only those who had an internal belief, and that kind of belief is not a lip confession but is a matter of the heart, and thus the life (AE 815).

Speak the Truth

Prayers also need to be honest. Did the father of the demon-possessed son speak the truth? Absolutely! "Lord, I believe; help my unbelief!" He had doubts, but he was coming down on the side of belief. That honesty opened up a window in his soul through which the Lord could enter.

We can say words that sound good, and on one level we even believe them. But prayer requires a deeper honesty. Since the Lord sees our intentions, the only prayers that can succeed are ones that reflect what we truly want and hope for. As the Lord teaches, "Truths with us are what pray, and we are continually in such prayers when we live according to truths" (AE 493e). Our prayers are more effective when we make sure that what we say reflects, as much as possible, what we actually believe.

Scripture offers some powerful examples of truthful prayer. One is the story of the Pharisee and the tax collector. The Pharisee offered a proud prayer: "God, I thank You that I am not like other people; extortioners, unjust, adulterers, or even as this tax collector. I fast twice a week; I give tithes of all that I possess." The tax collector offered a much more honest prayer: "God, be merciful to me, a sinner!" (Luke 18:9-14).

Believe That the Lord Is in Charge and Can Help

> *All things, whatever you ask in prayer, believing, you will receive.*
> *(Matt 21:22)*

The most common theme about prayer in the New Testament is that the Lord can respond to us when we have faith in Him (Matt 8:2-3, 8:5-8, 13, 22:21-22; John 14:12-14). The Lord did not say that we will get most things if we believe, but that we would receive "all things." The qualifier, of course, is that we believe in Him, which means we trust what He says enough to try to live it. And we trust that He will give us the things we really need, not what we think we need.

If we don't believe, we have no receptacle in ourselves for the Lord to act into. "The influx of the angels is into what a person knows and believes, but not into what a person does not know and does not believe; for their influx is not fixed anywhere except where there is something pertaining to the person" (AC 6206). There are many layers of belief, so we can expect to be peeling back layers of unbelief as we come to trust the Lord more and more throughout our lives.

"Ask, and It Will Be Given to You"

Even though we know the Lord is in charge and knows what we need better than we do, we still have to ask Him for help. In the Sermon on the Mount the Lord expresses that He wants to give us good things:

> Ask, and it will be given to you, seek and you will find, knock and it shall be opened to you. For everyone who asks receives, and he who seeks finds, and to him who knocks it will be opened. Or what man is there among you who if his child asks for bread will give him a stone? Or if he asks for a fish will he give him a serpent? If you then, being evil, know how to give good gifts to your children, how much more will your Father who is in heaven give good things to those who ask Him! (Matt 7:7-11)

This teaching offers a wonderful image of the Lord standing at the door knocking, waiting to give us good things, but requiring us to ask. He knows what we need better than we do, so why does He make us ask? The answer is that asking changes us: "It is common in all Divine worship for a person to first wish, desire, and pray, and for the Lord then to reply, instruct, and effect. A person does not otherwise accept anything Divine" (AR 376). We do not pray to change the Lord's mind. Rather, our willingness to ask, to receive, and to try to live what we ask for changes us and opens a door for Him (AE 248e).

Not only does the Lord already know what we should pray for, but when we are in a sincere state, He also gives us to know what to pray for (AR 376). It is beautiful to think that the process of turning to the Lord involves His guidance of us, not just in response to what we say, but in what to ask for in the first place. It shows how the Lord is actively engaging with us even before we start speaking.

Prayer for This Day

> *Give us this day our daily bread. (Matt 6:11)*

The Children of Israel were supposed to gather manna for only that one day. If they let it sit overnight, it would breed worms. Likewise, we cannot store up the benefits of prayer from one day to the next (LJP 337). We have no control over the past or the future; the only thing we can do anything about is the present. (See p. 122.) While we cannot change the past, we can honor, recognize, or change our attitude toward the past by our actions now. We *can* change the future but only by acting in the present moment. For example, we can't pray to the Lord to make us brave tomorrow. Tomorrow we will be in a different state and may not be open to being brave. What we can do is ask the Lord to fill us with courage now or to guide us to the correct decision right now. Focusing our prayers on what we need from the Lord today will keep us focused on the things that matter. "This is the day that the Lord has made. We will rejoice and be glad in it" (Ps 118:24).

Persistent Prayer Is Successful

While the Lord warns us against mindless repetition in prayer, He does encourage us to be intentionally persistent about praying for what is important to us. He tells the story of someone knocking on a friend's door at midnight to ask for supplies and having the door opened only because he is persistent:

> "I say to you, though he will not rise and give to him because he is his friend, yet because of his persistence he will rise and give him as many as he needs. So I say to you, ask, and it will be given to you; seek, and you will find; knock, and it will be opened to you.!" (Luke 11:8-10; see also Luke 18:1-8)

We might wonder why the Lord does not answer us right away but answers us only if we persist. As we have seen, prayer is not about changing God but about changing us. The point of persistence is to keep the issue in *our* minds and to invite the Lord into that issue, to turn the vessel of our mind to the Source of hope and change. The Lord sees what is needed in us that will allow Him in. Persistent prayer is one of the things that opens the pathway for Him to enter.

GETTING OUR HEARTS IN THE RIGHT PLACE

Let the words of my mouth and the meditation of my heart be pleasing before You, O Jehovah, my rock and my Redeemer. (Ps 19:14)

We have already seen that in prayer what is in our hearts matters more than what is in our mouth. Because of this, "angels pay no attention to anything else than the things that are internal—to ends in view, that is, to people's intentions and wills, and to their thoughts stemming from these" (AC 3489). Prayer is only as effective as the intention behind it (AE 325:3). It can seem daunting to keep our intentions pure, but the Lord offers guidance that can direct and comfort us.

Go to that inner place. The Lord says, "Enter into your bed chamber, and when you have shut the door, pray to your Father who is in secret" (Matt 6:6). Praying privately and sincerely does not necessarily mean being alone. It involves pulling within ourselves to figure out what we intend apart from what others think. In that private place we can offer our sincere commitments as well as share our fears.

Prayer from duty is okay. Sometimes we pray because we know we should even though we don't particularly feel like it. In certain periods of our lives, we may experience this quite often. Given how important our intention is in prayer, we may wonder if these prayers do any good. Swedenborg writes that they are useful: "I perceived that prayers to the Lord, if made from conscience, as a duty, are then good" (SE 3126). In fact, we might argue that praying when we do not feel like it reflects a deeper intention and is even more powerful than pouring forth prayers that come easily.

Prayer when we are not paying attention is okay. Anyone who prays knows that it is challenging to keep our minds on what we're saying, particularly when we're reciting a memorized prayer, such as the Lord's prayer. In fact, it can be easy to get through the prayer and realize that we have not thought about even one phrase of what we've said! This can be disheartening.

While we know the Lord wants us to pay attention when we pray, He also blesses our sincere but less-focused efforts. He knows our minds wander, and He does not expect perfection. He tells us that the prayers of children, who understand far less of what they are saying than adults do, are "much more fully heard in heaven than the prayers of grown-ups, and still more fully than those of people who have closed the way toward deeper things by thoughts of earthly matters and matters of memory" (SE 2435, 1826). Swedenborg also reports that "when I was paying less attention to the words of the Lord's prayer, the angels, I was told, understood them more fully" (SE 2435).

In essence, then, the willingness to "show up" to pray even when our minds wander allows the Lord to be present and to work with us. The choice to pray is the essential choice that opens us to Him.

WHAT CAN WE ASK FOR IN PRAYER?

We have seen that the Lord says, "All things, whatever you ask in prayer, believing, you will receive" (Matt 21:22). And we have seen that this does not mean that we will get whatever we want but rather that the Lord guides us to genuine prayer, which allows Him to answer our prayers affirmatively. The Lord offers guidance on the things we can pray for that make an affirmative response more likely.

Pray for Spiritual and Celestial Things

I do not pray that You should take them out of the world, but that You should keep them from the evil one. (John 17:9, 15)

The general teaching about what to ask for in prayer is that we should ask for interior things: "To those who are in a life of love and charity, what they are to ask is given from the Lord. Therefore they ask nothing but what is good, and that is done for them." (AE 325.8) "What is good" is defined even more in this passage:

A person who has faith from the Lord asks for nothing but what contributes to the Lord's kingdom and to the person's salvation. Other things he does not wish, saying in his heart, "Why should I ask for what does not contribute to this use?" (AE 815:10)

We are to ask for spiritually oriented things, and it is these requests the Lord was referring to when He said He would do "whatever" we ask in prayer, believing (Matt 21:12; AE 340).

When we pray, we often want some external situation to be fixed; we want to be taken out of the circumstances we are in. As the quote above says, the Lord's concerns are with helping us to deal with the issues we are facing and with protecting us from evil while we are doing so (John 17:9, 15). Since the Lord always prioritizes eternal qualities in us, He may offer us help that does not solve the external problem but rather gives us the will or the insight to deal with it gracefully.

Why Asking for Material Things Does Not Work

Some people have said that you should ask the Lord for everything. After all, what could possibly be bad about asking the Lord for help with all our concerns, including material ones? Here is a teaching that offers some guidance:

The Lord hears everyone and so brings help to everyone, but each according to that person's needs. Those who cry out to Him and call for help solely in support of themselves, and so in opposition to others, as the evil are accustomed to do, are also heard by the Lord, but He does not bring them help. When He does not bring help, it is said that He does not hear. (AC 6852)

We may rarely ask the Lord to support us directly at the expense of other people. The challenge is that when we ask for something that is finite, we are often in effect asking that others won't get it. "Let my team win this game" means we are praying that the other team will lose. "Let me get this job" means other people won't. It's the same with any finite resource.

How, then, can we pray for anything that has worldly implications? In interviewing for a job, we could pray that we will do our best, or we could pray that the Lord will create the best possible outcome (which might mean that we don't get the job). We might pray that we become the kind of person who is worthy and able to do that job. We might pray for courage or that we convey an open and willing spirit in the interview. All these things do not take away from anyone else's happiness because they are things the Lord can give in infinite measure. And they do not ensure the outcome that we want; they require our trusting that the Lord knows how best to answer.

In the end, how successful we are in purely worldly terms, however important that may be to us now, is not very important to the Lord. He wants something different: "Seek first the kingdom of God and His justice, and all these things will be added to you" (Matt 6:33). If we are willing to ask Him for what is eternal, He will give us what we need in this world, even if it is not exactly what we think we need (AC 8478).

An Important Qualifier for Each Request

Sometimes we can be unsure whether what we want to ask for is okay. Our instinct in that situation might be to avoid asking in case it's for the wrong thing. But we should take the opposite approach. When in doubt, ask, but in a qualified way. In the Garden of Gethsemane, the Lord said, "Father, if it is possible, let this cup pass from Me. Nevertheless, not as I will, but as You will" (Matt 26:39). From His merely human state, He asked for what He wanted but then left things in the hands of His Divine soul, just as we might ask for what we want but then leave things up to the Lord. As another teaching says, "In prayer, when inspired by God, there is always the thought and belief that the Lord alone knows whether what is sought would be beneficial or not. Therefore the one who prays leaves the Lord to decide whether to listen to what he asks for, then accordingly pleads that the Lord's will may be done, not his own" (AC 8179:4). Perhaps we could end every prayer with a qualifier: "Nevertheless, not as I will but as You will."

ANSWERS TO PRAYER

> *Call to Me, and I will answer you, and show you great and mighty things, which you do not know. (Jer 33:3)*

> *It shall come to pass that before they call, I will answer; and while they are still speaking, I will hear. (Is 65:24)*

We have addressed how to pray, and now we will consider how to discern the Lord's answers to our prayers. If prayer is talking with God, then presumably He is "talking" back to us in some fashion. Perhaps what frustrates people most about prayer is that discerning the answer can be difficult. We can crave a tangible answer. As the quotes above show, the Lord says that He will answer our prayers if we call out to Him. Clearly He does not mean this literally, so we need to explore what the Lord does and does not mean.

The Lord answers prayers in three ways. First, when a prayer is truly from Him, He often answers us by *giving us aid* for what we are trying to accomplish—the strength and courage to carry on, the compassion to answer mildly, the forbearance not to retaliate, the integrity to speak truthfully and sincerely (see AE 471:2e). Often we will find that we have just enough of whatever quality we need to get through, just as Elijah and the widow of Zarephath had just enough oil and flour each day to have food until the famine ended (1 Kings 17:8-16). The Lord allows us to feel that we have just enough energy and insight because this feeling forces us to make a choice, to dig deep to choose what's right, all the while acknowledging that the strength to do so came from the Lord (AC 10299:4).

Second, in answer to our prayers He responds with "*something like a revelation*, which is manifested in the affection of the one who prays as hope, consolation, or a certain inward joy" (AC 2535). This means that He guides us by the affections He inspires. We may notice these as hope that a challenge can be overcome, consolation after a major struggle, or inward joy at something good we observe in our lives. In other words, the Lord guides our heart in a way that clarifies things for us.

Finally, at the same time as He touches our hearts, He *gives us more direct perceptions of what is true* (see AE 471:2). He causes us to see things we had not seen before. Perhaps you have prayed to the Lord and had a thought you'd not had before that challenged you or caused you to rethink what you were asking for. That could easily be a perception from the Lord. We need to be paying attention to notice this gentle answer.

Asking Questions the Lord Can Answer in Ways We Can Hear

Since the Lord answers us by means of a perception of the truth, we need to understand what perception is. The Lord tells us that the highest angels have a perception of truth that we do not have. It is an immediate insight into the truth or falsity of something when they contemplate it:

> From perception they know instantly whether something is so or not so. Consequently when any statement about faith is made, their response is either "That is so," or "That is not so," for they are perceiving from the Lord. This is what the Lord's words mean in Matthew, "Let your words be, 'Yes, Yes,' 'No, No'; anything beyond this is from evil."—Matt. 5:37 (AC 202)

This perception is not as much a general insight into a question the angels may have (though that can happen) as it is a knowing "whether something is so or not so."

We cannot have perception in the way celestial angels do or as the ancients did, but we can have elements of it if we offer the Lord a scenario which He can answer with "Yes" or "No." For example, the Lord would be less able to give a specific answer to a general prayer for guidance in finding an eternal partner. Nor would He be able to clearly answer a question such as "Who should I marry?" But if someone were to say, "I think I should marry this person. Does that have your blessing?" that is a yes/no question that the Lord can answer with a perception we can sense.

Since one of the ways the Lord answers us is by guiding our affections and giving us a sense of hope, consolation, or inward joy, we can ask the Lord a specific question in humble prayer and observe how He guides our affections. In our example about finding a partner, if we were to feel hope or joy at the thought of marrying a certain someone after praying about it, we might have more confidence that the Lord can bless that decision. But if we felt sadness or unease, that feeling might lead us to a different decision. Even such a specific prayer may need to be offered persistently over time for us to get a sense of the Lord's guidance.

Prayers the Lord Cannot Answer

Sometimes we ask for things in prayer that the Lord cannot answer affirmatively because He is always focused on eternal benefits. Here are some examples of prayers He cannot answer.

When answering means someone else would suffer. As we have seen (p. 83), the Lord cannot give us many material things that we ask for because in a finite world our receiving it means someone else does not. In general, the Lord cannot answer indirect prayers that someone else not get something because that would be doing evil. Prayers to win the game, to win the lottery, to get the job, to be chosen for a part in a play are not prayers the Lord can answer positively.

During temptation and other times when we want to be rescued. When we are engaged in a spiritual struggle, we are more likely than at any other time to turn to the Lord. Yet it is one of the times the Lord is least likely to answer our prayers, at least in the way we would like. The Lord sees that we benefit more from going through the process of temptation than being rescued from it.

When the Lord was arrested, one of the people with Him "drew his sword, struck the servant of the high priest, and cut off his ear." The Lord responded that He could ask for twelve legions of angels if He wanted to. He concluded, "How then could the Scriptures be fulfilled, that it must happen thus?" (Matt 26:47-54).

He knew that the only way to end His struggle was to go through it. This is why the Lord does not answer prayers in temptation:

> When people are in the throes of temptation, they usually stop moving their hands and resort solely to prayers, which they then pour forth feverishly, unaware that such prayers achieve nothing, but that they should battle against the falsities and evils which the hells introduce.... In the conflicts brought by temptations, we should fight as if we did so in our own strength, yet we should acknowledge and believe that we do so in the Lord's.... Moreover, people in the throes of temptation who take no action other than to send up prayers do not realize that if their temptation were terminated before running its full course, their preparation for heaven would not be accomplished, and so they could not be saved. For this reason also little heed is paid to the prayers of those in the throes of temptation, for the Lord desires the end in view, which is the person's salvation. (AC 8179:2, 3)

Ultimately, the Lord answers our true request—that we find happiness and peace. But He answers it for the long term by allowing us to walk through the valley of the shadow of death. In the short term we may wonder if we are heard.

When the answer is No. Sometimes we think a prayer has gone unanswered when in reality the answer was no. Over our lifetime we ask for many things, often for changes or for things that we believe will make us happy. If we are living well, the Lord answers our real request, which is that we be happy. And the way to make us happiest may be to say no to a prayer we ask in the short term.

A song from the early 90s by Garth Brooks called "Unanswered Prayers" illustrates this. It is a true account of his own experience of running into his high school sweetheart when he and his wife were at a football game. He remembers that he had prayed to God to make this other woman his. But now, looking at his wife, he could not be more grateful that God had not answered that earlier prayer. The song ends with this line: "Some of God's greatest gifts are unanswered prayers."

The Lord always answers prayers. Our job is to ask for things He can answer affirmatively.

THE IMPORTANCE OF PRAYER FOR OTHERS

For some, prayer for others is an uncomfortable topic. They say that since the Lord knows what everyone needs, He does not need us to tell Him, and it can seem presumptuous to do so.

Yet the Word shows us that the Lord wants us to pray for others. In the Lord's prayer we pray for others. We say, "Give *us* this day our daily bread," "Forgive *us* our debts," "Lead *us* not into temptation." When we say this prayer, most of us probably think about our own spiritual needs, and that is appropriate. At times it might be useful to say that prayer as a gift to those we love. Or we could pray for everyone in church with us or everyone in our family, emphasizing the communal nature of the Lord's prayer.

The Lord also tells us directly to pray for others: "The harvest truly is plentiful, but the laborers are few. Therefore pray the Lord of the harvest to send out laborers into His harvest" (Matt 9:37-38). The inner meaning of this is that we are to pray that the Lord's kingdom may come (AR 956), in effect praying that people will do things that will bring the Lord's kingdom to earth.

The Lord's teaching about prayer for others is even more direct in the Sermon on the Mount:

> You have heard that it was said, "You shall love your neighbor and hate your enemy." But I say to you, love your enemies, bless those who curse you, do good to those who hate you, and pray for those who spitefully use you and persecute you, that you may be sons of your Father in heaven. (Matt 5:43-46)

The Lord supports this literal teaching by explaining that the inner meaning is about looking to the good of another, even an enemy. To pray for them means to intercede on their behalf (AE 644:23).

The need to pray for others is stated most clearly in the following passage: "There are those who think they deserve heaven because of their earnest prayers. *Yet they do not pray for others, still less for everyone, but only for themselves. Thus their prayers are not heard*, except perhaps in earthly matters" (SE 1850). Prayers for ourselves are not heard unless we are also praying for others!

We see, then, that praying for others is not useless, nor is it merely a good optional activity. Rather, it is an essential act we all need to engage in, a powerful force for good in the world.

PRAY EVEN FOR THOSE WHO HAVE HURT YOU

Praying for the good in others is a pleasant idea. But what about praying for enemies or for those who have hurt us? Since only the Lord is perfect, everyone else we interact with is going to hurt us at some point. Sometimes they will even do so with the full intention of causing us pain. Our instinct says that when people act that way, it is okay to feel resentment and even to hate them. Yet the Lord says the opposite. Just as on the cross He forgave those who reviled and killed Him, He tells us to forgive, which is hard. And He also tells us that we should pray for those who have hurt us:

> You have heard that it was said, 'You shall love your neighbor and hate your enemy.' But I say to you, love your enemies, bless those who curse you, do good to those who hate you, and pray for those who spitefully use you and persecute you,

that you may be sons of your Father in heaven; for He makes His sun rise on the evil and on the good, and sends rain on the just and on the unjust. For if you love those who love you, what reward have you? Do not even the tax collectors do the same? (Matt 5:43-46)

This is strong teaching! Bless those who curse you. Pray for those who spitefully use you and persecute you. Love your enemies.

Think for a moment about what happens when we feel hurt. We are usually caught up in replaying the painful scene, trying to find fierce words that we wish we had said to fight back or justifying what we did say. We steep ourselves in this toxic brew that holds within it the quality of wishing harm on someone. In essence, we curse that person in our mind, returning evil for evil. By contrast, the Lord says to pray, bless, love. Instead of heaping evil on that person in our minds (and thereby bringing it on ourselves), we can look for the good in that person and hope and pray that they find peace from whatever drove them to hurt us.

The Lord teaches extensively about the need for rising above resentments and praying for others. We'll explore this teaching more deeply, but for now I invite you to let the literal meaning and the emotional tone of this teaching sink in.

> But I say to you who hear: Love your enemies, do good to those who hate you, bless those who curse you, and pray for those who spitefully use you. To him who strikes you on the one cheek, offer the other also. And from him who takes away your cloak, do not withhold your tunic either. Give to everyone who asks of you. And from him who takes away your goods do not ask them back. And just as you want people to do to you, you also do to them likewise. But if you love those who love you, what credit is that to you? For even sinners love those who love them. And if you do good to those who do good to you, what credit is that to you? For even sinners do the same. And if you lend to those from whom you hope to receive back, what credit is that to you? For even sinners lend to sinners to receive as much back. But love your enemies, do good, and lend, hoping for nothing in return; and your reward will be great, and you will be sons of the Most High. For He is kind to the unthankful and evil. Therefore be merciful, just as your Father also is merciful. Judge not, and you shall not be judged. Condemn not, and you shall not be condemned. Forgive, and you will be forgiven. Give, and it will be given to you: good measure, pressed down, shaken together, and running over will be put into your bosom. For with the same measure that you use, it will be measured back to you. (Luke 6:27-38)

All of us have been hurt by others, yet we are told to pray for those who have hurt us. Strange as it may seem, we need to pray for others for our own protection. Praying for someone when they have hurt us is a gift far above what we may feel like giving. We are to turn the other cheek, meaning that we to choose not to match hate with hate:

Internal people, as the angels of heaven are, do not wish to retaliate to evil by evil, but from heavenly charity they forgive freely. For they know that the Lord protects all who are in good from the evil, that He protects according to the good with them, and that He would not protect if on account of the evil done to them they should burn with enmity, hatred, and revenge, for these drive away protection. Angels do not fight with the evil, much less do they return evil for evil, but they allow it to be done, since they are protected by the Lord, and therefore no evil from hell can do them harm. (AE 556:9)

This is a non-intuitive teaching. The protection and safety of the angels lies not in defending themselves against external harm, but in not matching hate with hate. Part of the reason we pray for those who have hurt us is to protect our own souls from being dragged into hell because of our response to what others have done. By praying we assert that we are spiritual beings and that our essence is under the Lord's care alone. Though others can harm our bodies and external spirits they cannot harm our essential selves.

What is more, praying for those who treat us well means little unless we are also willing to pray for those who are more challenging to pray for. The Lord says that even evil people love and pray for those who love them back. That's more of a bargain than a prayer. By praying for others who do not love us back, we make prayer the spiritual act it is rather than a negotiation.

When we choose not to forgive people who have treated us badly, the underlying anger and hatred sabotages our prayer life and our efforts to help others. Hard as it is, in our prayer life we need to pay attention to forgiving others, even to the point of wishing good to those who do not treat us well.[1] As the Lord says, "If you bring your gift to the altar and there remember that your brother has something against you, leave your gift there before the altar, and go your way. First be reconciled with your brother, and then come and offer your gift" (Matt 5:23-24).

What it comes down to is this: If we want forgiveness and compassion when we make mistakes, we are called to give them. In the above passage from Luke, the Lord gives us the Golden Rule in this context of dealing with people who don't treat us well. We can ask ourselves how we would want to be treated at times when we do harm to someone. We would need that person to pray for us and so to do good to us. And because we need that, when someone hurts us, we need to pray for them and do good to them.

The quotation above from Luke 6 ends:

---

[1]The Lord is not saying that we should forgive blindly and let people walk all over us. That is unkind and unjust, both to ourselves and to those we allow to mistreat us. Rather, we need to let go of the hatred and resentment that the hells inject into our unforgiving feelings even as we take clear stands when appropriate.

> Therefore be merciful, just as your Father also is merciful. Judge not, and you shall not be judged. Condemn not, and you shall not be condemned. Forgive, and you will be forgiven. Give, and it will be given to you: good measure, pressed down, shaken together, and running over will be put into your bosom. For with the same measure that you use, it will be measured back to you. (Luke 6:36-38)

The message is clear: We get what we give. When we give, we will receive a full measure from the Lord. When we hold resentments, we offer a tiny measure to the Lord that He fills, but it does not satisfy us. By praying for others who have hurt us, we not only do them a service, but we also offer a big measure to the Lord. We open ourselves up to the great blessings that He is offering to us in return.

When we pray for others who have hurt us, then, we engage in a central battle for our own souls. By being willing to forgive the people who have hurt us and wish them well, we will have learned to love in a truly spiritual way.

PULLING IT TOGETHER

If we want to love the Lord and have a relationship with Him, we have to be talking to Him and listening for His response. Since He already knows what we are thinking and feeling, we can offer our unfiltered thoughts and wishes to Him. We don't need to pretend to be better than we are or hide problems that exist; there's no point. Instead, we can sincerely talk to Him and ask for His help, knowing that He always sees with eyes of true love and justice.

Prayer is most effective when we believe that the Lord knows what we need and we are willing to open ourselves to whatever direction He may offer. When we do this, we allow our prayers to spring from His guidance, which means they will be successful prayers.

Prayer is not about changing the Lord's mind but about changing our hearts so we can receive His blessings. We need to pray persistently because by being persistent we come to care about what we are asking for. And because prayer is about changing our hearts, we need to turn to the Lord for help with heavenly, eternal things, not for worldly things, especially not for worldly things that would be taken away from someone else.

In addition to praying for ourselves, we need to pray for other people. In fact, our prayers for our own personal development can be heard only to the extent to which we pray for others, including our enemies!

ACTIVITIES AND QUESTIONS

1. What is your experience with prayer? When has prayer been easy? When has it been a challenge?

2. If you do not already, consider embracing the idea of praying morning and evening. Then add in meals and any other time you feel a need. If you are married, consider praying with your spouse at least one of those times.

3. What is a spiritual need right now? Over the course of the next week, ask the Lord's help daily in overcoming it.

4. Pray for someone else's well-being this week.

5. Who do you consider an enemy, or at least someone you don't particularly like? See if you can pray sincerely for that person's well-being.

6. Build some time into your day or week to pray and then stop to listen, as it were, for the Lord's guidance in response to your prayer.

7. The Lord said, "It is written, My house shall be called a house of prayer..." (Matt 21:13). How might we make prayer a more prominent part of our church and community life?

Read the Word and Other Spiritual Books

Your Word is a lamp to my feet and a light for my path. (Ps 119:105)

No one can be introduced into the church and formed for heaven except by means of concepts from the Word. (AE 112:3)

True order is for a person to become wise from the Lord, that is, from His Word. (AC 129)

Everything of value we have explored so far in this book has come from the Word, and every meaningful movement in our life needs to be guided by truths from the Word. In our daily life we focus on the issue at hand, which is good and right. But even then the truths of the Word show us the path and guide us on it.

As the teachings just above indicate, the Lord wants us to delight in turning to Him in His Word because the Word is an essential means for us to get to heaven. This chapter explores why it important to read the Word and then provides some guidance on how to go about reading it.

Before we begin, I should note that when I refer to the Word I am referring to the Old and New Testaments and Swedenborg's Writings. All of them are the Word though in different ways.

WE NEED TO KNOW A LOT ABOUT SPIRITUAL LIVING

These days many people focus on fundamental truths such as the Golden Rule and the Ten Commandments, sometimes to the point of saying that we really don't need to know much more. We are told to "just love people." Part of us wants it to be that simple, and in some ways it is that simple.

Yet keeping things simple, while it sounds appealing, can also be limiting and even dangerous. People with no knowledge of truth can have no faith; those with few truths can have a "weak and impoverished" faith; and those with a lot of knowledge can have a faith that is "rich and full according to their number" (Faith 28). In fact, "what people know nothing about is unintelligible to them even if it happens to them" (AC 5365:3; see also 5649:3). We can look back at times when we were confused about what was happening in our lives, yet now, using knowledge that we did not have then, we understand those events more clearly. As the Lord says elsewhere, "What we do not know, we cannot think about, and thus cannot will, therefore neither can we believe or love" (AE 112:3). As long as we use what we know, more knowledge is helpful, and even essential (see AC 2189, 3324).

Not only do we benefit from ongoing learning, but it is actually essential to spiritual living:

> The situation in the spiritual world is that those there satisfy their hunger with truths and goods, for they constitute the food of those there. But once that food has served its purpose, those people enter a further state of dearth. It is like the nourishing of a person with material food, in that once this food has served its purpose, that person begins to feel hungry again. (AC 5579)

We learn a truth at a certain time and in a certain state of mind. It serves us well and then becomes something we lose awareness of. In a year or two, we may run across that same truth and find that it strikes us totally differently and feeds us in a new way. This is why we need to be continuously learning from the Word (see DP 172:5).

WHY READING THE WORD FOR TRUTH IS IMPORTANT

When we have grown up with the Word, our familiarity with it can mean it loses some of the special quality we once felt it to have. And if we've not grown up with it, we may never have had that feeling in the first place. Yet the Word is a special, holy work, and reading it is deeply important. Here are some reasons why this is so. You can read more about them in *Exploring the Path*, 223-231.

- The Lord tells us to.
- The Lord alone teaches us in the Word.
- We see the Lord in the truths of the Word.
- The Word is Divine Truth with us.
- The Word is the only source of real truth, and it opens heaven to us.
- We cannot know what good is apart from truths from the Word.
- The Lord can dwell with us only in what is His own.
- Discovering the truth for ourselves sets us free.
- The Lord tells us to read the Word so we can verify or reject the teaching of our church.
- We experience the Lord when we read the Word.

Taken as a whole, we see that reading the Word gives us a more direct connection and relationship with the Lord as well as the essential truth we need to succeed in our spiritual journey.

MOTIVES MAKE A DIFFERENCE

Therefore with joy you will draw water from the wells of salvation.
(Is 12:3)

More than with any other book we read, our attitude toward the Word makes an enormous difference to what we get out of it. When we read a scientific work, our attitude toward that work and the author matters. If we are doubtful about the author, we are less likely to agree with what he or she says. The attitude we hold when we read the Word is much more important because in addition to affecting our openness to the ideas there, our attitude is the means by which we access the truths of the Word. It seems the Lord has built a protective measure into the Word such that we will not see much truth in it unless we genuinely want to. We're told that many people "put a lot of effort into reading" the Word, but they "cling to their own dogmas, and are anxious only to confirm these from the Word" (AC 4368:2). As we might imagine, their great effort will not lead to much insight. When we read the Word, our motives and attitude are primary considerations.

The most powerful motive for reading the Word is a desire to be guided by the Lord. "People who read [the Word] from the Lord, and not from themselves alone, are filled by it with the good arising from love and the truths of wisdom" (SS 3). That means we are reading with a humble desire to find truth, not because we are intelligent or because we are diligent, but because we are turning to the Lord. We do not "conquer" reading the Word so much as we surrender ourselves to the truth.

Our willingness to read from the Lord is particularly important when we want to understand the spiritual meaning of the Word.

We cannot see the spiritual sense except from the Lord alone, and unless we are in Divine truths from the Lord.... We can violate Divine Truth, if we have a knowledge of correspondences and by it proceed to explore the spiritual sense of the Word from our own intelligence. This is because by a few correspondences known to us we may pervert the spiritual meaning, and even force it to confirm what is false. This would be to offer violence to Divine Truth, and also to heaven. Therefore, if we desire to discover that sense from ourselves and not from the Lord, heaven is closed to us. When heaven is closed, we either see no truth or become spiritually insane. (SS 26)

This is a strong statement that shows how much our attitude toward the Lord's presence in the Word changes our experience in reading it.

The most commonly mentioned motive that affects our ability to receive truth is the affection for truth for the sake of truth (AC 8993:4, 5432:4, 9382:2, 177:3;

Verbo 12; AE 115, 117, 923:2). We can seek truth for many other reasons: for the sake of power, financial gain, or position (AC 3769:3, 5432:2, 4); for the sake of reputation (AC 3769:3); to provide confirmation for what we want to see (AC 5432:4, 4368:2); from curiosity (Verbo 12); or from force of habit (AC 3769:3). To the extent that we rise above these motivations and search for truth for its own sake, the Lord's light will shine in our minds, and we will understand what we read.

The general teaching is that "everyone's affection receives and takes in things congenial to itself, as a sponge absorbs water. Thus the spiritual affection for truth receives and takes in spiritual truths" (AE 118:2). When we don't see anything in the Word, the most likely reason is that there is not a correlation between what is in us already and the truth that is in the Word in great abundance.[1] Because we are flawed human beings, this is something we should expect and be gentle with ourselves about. In fact, the whole reason to read the Word is that we're not perfect. Our challenge as we read is to do it with curiosity and a desire to learn. Sometimes reading can seem like a chore; then a sentence will jump out at us, and an affection will be sparked. Once that affection is active, we may see many exciting truths for the rest of our reading.

We know from experience that different affections can be active in us at different times and sometimes even at the same time. We can't always help having lower motives. But we can intentionally ask the Lord to guide our hearts to read the Word from a love for the truths that are there. To the extent that that affection is present, the Word will be open to us.

Innocence is at the heart of an affection for truth for the sake of truth. We can access what it means to read the Word with innocence by thinking about the innocence of children. Many of us have had a child eagerly tell us some new piece of information that he or she has learned. The information may be commonly known, such as the fact that butterflies were once "worms" that built a house for themselves so they could turn into beautiful flying creatures. The child is full of joy because of this new discovery, and this joy in a result of innocence.

As adults we can emulate that childlike quality. We can be open to new ideas, to the truth. When we are open like a child is, we are willing to be led and taught. That innocence, or openness, leads to the joy of discovery and to new ideas.

Think about what a child knows compared to an adult. In spiritual matters we are like children compared to the Lord. If we pick up the Lord's Word with the attitude of being His child and open ourselves up to what He has to teach us, we create the possibility of that joyful discovery that every child experiences.

---

[1] Other factors may make the Word hard to understand, such as lacking the requisite knowledge, or being sick or tired.

Another aspect of being childlike is not to expect too much. We might expect that we will be able to read the Word and gain great insights. It doesn't always happen that way. Sometimes we learn little things or things that many other people have already learned. The childlike part in us can delight in each new idea.

This childlike quality of innocence is the key motive we need in reading the Word. The Lord tells us that because of their mutual love and innocence, angels receive more insight when children read the Word than when adults who do not live the truth do. Similarly, the Word is made alive according to our degree of innocence (AC 1776, 3690).

When we read the Word from an affection for truth and innocence, there is no guarantee that we will see the truth without error. Because we are imperfect, we invariably accept false ideas as true, or we take a generally true idea and apply it in particular ways that are inappropriate and therefore false. Yet because the Lord focuses on our intentions, if they are good, He is able to use even our false ideas for good:

> It should be recognized that no falsity as such ... can be made our own if we are governed by good and therefore wish to know the truth, only when we are ruled by evil and therefore have no wish to know the truth. The reason ... is that [those governed by good] think in a proper way about God, about God's kingdom, and about spiritual life, and therefore use falsity in such a way that it is not at odds with them but somehow in agreement. Thus they soften it, and none of its harshness or hardness enters their ideas. (AC 8051)

The Lord offers us wonderful protection by leading us to use falsity in a way that is not at odds with spiritual principles or by softening our use of a false idea so that it is less harmful. This is a powerful illustration of the leading principle of this section, namely, that motives are the most important factor in our ability to be led to see truth.

BARRIERS TO READING THE WORD

> *On hearing it, many of His disciples said, "This is a hard teaching. Who can accept it?" ... From that time many of His disciples went back and walked with Him no more. Then Jesus said to the twelve, "Do you also want to go away?" But Simon Peter answered Him, "Lord, to whom shall we go? You have the words of eternal life." (John 6:60, 66-68)*

Sometimes the Word appears to have flaws, and these flaws can cause us to ignore it or to reject it. We want to find the Lord in it, but part of our mind ends up objecting to the things we read, or we feel confused. There are three apparent flaws that can bother us: The Word doesn't seem particularly special; it seems can be to understand; and the Lord appears cruel, arbitrary, or unfair in it. The Lord teaches how we can think about these barriers and rise above them.

The Word Doesn't Seem Particularly Special

We know that the Word was written by God and that it therefore contains all wisdom. Yet it does not appear that way. "In its letter the Word appears like common writing, unfamiliar in style, appearing neither as sublime nor as brilliant as the writings of the present day" (SS 1). Because of this we could easily "hold it in contempt, and say to ourselves when we read it, 'What is this? What is that? Is this Divine? Can God, whose wisdom is infinite, speak in this way? Where and from what source comes its holiness except from religious belief and consequently from conviction?'" (SS 1).

What is more, Swedenborg was aware that some looked at his writings the same way. He reports that some spirits, caught in the same external thinking, said that "the things I have written are so crude, so coarse, that they consider nothing to be understandable from these words, or the mere meaning of the words" (SE 2185). Self-help books and the like can appear to be more helpful and powerfully written.

There is a Divine plan behind the way the Lord gave us the Word. Without those seemingly "crude" outer meanings, inwardly "clean and holy" matters could not be contained. The crude outer meanings allow the Lord to reach the simplest people while the deeper meanings can reach the most spiritual and thoughtful (SE 2185). That is a marvelous miracle.

Because of the way it is written, the Word also offers a protection mechanism: "The writing [in the Word] is such that it shines brightly before those who believe in the Lord and in the new revelation; but it appears dark and of no consequence to those who deny them, and who are not in favor of them on account of various external reasons" (Eccl Hist 4). The Word is something like a Rorschach ink blot. We see in it what is in us—simple truths if we are just beginning to read, profound truth if we have an affection for it, and crude babbling if we are not interested.[1] We tend to see only what we are ready to see, and we are unlikely to take in truths that we are unwilling to live and would therefore falsify, thereby doing further harm to our souls.

---

[1] At times the Word will seem confusing or hard to understand for anyone, but that is different from taking a dismissive attitude toward confusing passages.

It Seems Too Hard to Understand

Sometimes the Word, particularly the Heavenly Doctrines, seems to be written for scholars and theologians—too erudite for "normal" people. This complaint is probably the most common objection people make to reading the Word. They say it is too far above them, and they can't understand it. There is some truth to this observation if we consider that the Word was written for all people and angels and for all time. The Lord wrote it in such a way that the simplest people can get what they need, and the wisest can study for eternity and still find more truths every day. We can reasonably expect some sections of the Word to speak primarily to states beyond ours though many sections are clear, simple, and understandable to all.

It can be a novel idea that it is okay not to understand, and in fact it is an important one: "People moved by a spiritual affection for truth perceive that there are few things which they know, and infinitely numerous things which they do not know. They know also that to know and acknowledge this is the first step to wisdom" (AE 117:2). With awareness of our limitations comes the acknowledgment "in heart that we of ourselves know nothing, that we have neither understanding nor wisdom, but that all knowledge, understanding, and wisdom are from the Lord" (AE 118). We might say that at times the Lord allows us not to understand the Word because that lack of understanding leads us toward this first step to wisdom. The humility of spirit in us that recognizes how little we know will also lead us to be open to learning more.

Even though at times we will struggle to comprehend it, the Lord wants us to understand His Word: "Every person whose soul so desires can see the truths of the Word in light" (TCR 621:3). Or to put in another way, "Everyone—no matter who, provided that he is not mentally deficient—is endowed with ... the ability to understand whether things are true" (AC 5464:2). Perhaps it is fair to say that though there will be things we don't understand, the Lord will always give us enough understanding to take the next step in our spiritual life.

We might consider it ironic that people object to the Word as being both simple and crude, and intellectual and deep. If the objections were only on one side or the other, they might have more merit. But the accusation of both simplicity and complexity suggests that the Word is written as it is on purpose, with a range of meanings suitable for all to gain wisdom.

The Lord Appears Cruel, Arbitrary, or Unfair

Another barrier is that the Lord appears angry, vindictive, arbitrary, cruel, capricious, or unfair in the Word. We know these are not characteristics of a Divinely loving God, and it can be hard to read the Word with a sense of its holiness when we come across such stories.

There is a teaching that clarifies why the Word is written with these images. It says that the literal sense is written to reflect the way things appear to us from the outside while the inner meaning describes what actually happens in spiritual reality (AC 1310). For example, when the children of Israel do something wrong and the Lord appears angry, that reflects the fact that when we choose evil, the consequences of that choice feel like the Lord is punishing us (see AC 357). Children who are being punished feel that their parents are angry at them when in fact the parents may look stern on the outside but grieving on the inside.

A principle at work here is that general concepts have to come before the details. Sometimes the most general idea is not intuitively obvious to us. Consider this teaching about why the Lord allows Himself to be portrayed as angry and punishing when in fact He is never angry:

> Jehovah God or the Lord never curses anyone, is never angry with anyone, never leads anyone into temptation, and never punishes, let alone curses anybody. It is the devil's crew who do such things. Such things cannot possibly come from the fountain of mercy, peace, and goodness. The reason why ... in the Word it is said that Jehovah God not only turns His face away, is angry, punishes, and tempts, but also slays and even curses, is that people may believe that the Lord rules over and disposes every single thing in the whole world, including evil itself, punishments, and temptations. And after people have grasped this very general concept, they may then learn in what ways He rules and disposes, and how He converts into good the evil inherent in punishment and the evil inherent in temptation. In teaching and learning the Word, very general concepts have to come first; and therefore the sense of the letter is full of such general concepts. (AC 245)

The underlying reality is that the Lord is always loving no matter how things may appear, but because He needs to be seen as in charge, sometimes He allows Himself to be portrayed in less accurate ways. If we can keep this idea in mind, we can maintain some perspective when we come to hard stories in the Word.

Even more importantly, as we develop the qualities of love and compassion in ourselves, we will readily see them in the Lord. The Lord says, "To the merciful I will show myself merciful" (2 Sam 22:26) and "Blessed are the pure in heart, for they shall see God" (Matt 5:8). Yet again, we see that what we bring to the reading of the Word influences what we get out of.

BENEFITS OF READING THE WORD

These things I have spoken to you, that My joy may remain in you, and
that your joy may be full. (John 15:11)

We know, in a broad sense, that reading the Word is good for us. But what specific
benefits accrue to us when we take time to sit down and open the Word? Some of
the ideas that follow may be familiar, but they are important enough to stop and
ponder because each one of them is deeply valuable.

The Lord Is Present

The presence of the Lord and heaven exists everywhere the Word is read
reverently. (DP 260:3)

The greatest gift we can receive is to become aware of the Lord in our lives. He is
the source of peace, hope, joy, and life. That life flows into us when we read the
Word because inmostly the Word treats of the Lord and in fact is the Lord (AC
3424:2).

> The Word is Divine Truth from the Lord, which deals in its highest sense with the
> Lord alone. All this being so, those who receive enlightenment when they read the
> Word see the Lord; they do so because of the faith and the love they have. They
> see Him solely in the Word and in no other writing whatever. (AC 9411)

Holiness Is Present

The Word is holy (AC 8971), and as we might expect, reading it allows that holiness
to affect us. We are affected by its holiness when we read (AC 10402:6, 10635) even
though we are often unaware of it (HD 256; AC 10635). In fact, "the holiness which
fills us possesses countless facets concealed within it which we do not see" (AC
5466). While we might not notice the holiness with us, I suspect we would notice
if it were gone.

The Lord Teaches Us

The most obvious benefit of reading is that we learn things. "When the Word is
being read, the Lord flows in and teaches" (AC 6516:3). He does not just teach us
general truths but "as it were gives answers, when truth is sought from the heart's
affection, and when it is loved as good" (AC 9905:4). He addresses the concerns
that we have. Many of us have had the experience of reading the Word only to find

that the section we are reading directly relates to something going on in our life. While this may seem like a coincidence, it is not. There is infinite truth in anything we read, and when we read with questions in mind, whether we are conscious of them or not, we are open to the answers the Lord gives to those questions.

When the Lord teaches us, He offers us insight by means of enlightenment. All of us have the Lord's light shining in our minds even when we are in a state of evil (AE 140:6-7). This light allows us to change because it shines independent of the choices of our will. There is also a deeper enlightenment that shines into our minds when our hearts are open to it (AC 9382:2):

> [This light] enlightens the minds of people ... and enables them to understand truth and also to perceive good when they read the Word from the Lord and not from self. They are then living in connection with angels and interiorly have perception like the spiritual perception of angels. That spiritual perception which a person-angel has flows into his or her natural perception. (AE 1067:3)

When we are enlightened in this way, our spirits deep within us actually have the perception of angels. That heavenly clarity then filters into our natural consciousness and illuminates our thought. This explains why the Lord's Word can offer amazing inspiration at some times and very little at others. Our hearts can, at times, open us to angelic insight.

We Expand Our Spiritual Connections

The teaching about enlightenment shows us how reading the Word enhances the depth of our spiritual insights. Reading also expands not only the breadth of our knowledge but also the breadth of our spiritual connections, which in turn extends the reach of our thoughts. To understand this, we need to think about the concept of our spiritual home.

Each of us is connected with a community of angels or devils based on our deepest loves, and in fact we receive our life and our thoughts through that community (AC 4067:2). Our thoughts and affections are intimately connected to where we are in the spiritual world, which is why it makes sense when we describe a bad mood as "being in a bad place." In our spirits, each of us has actually been in heaven and in hell many times. And each of us lives primarily in some specific heavenly or hellish community that most reflects what we love. Because that is our spiritual home, it is the lens through which we see everything. Only by the gradual work of allowing the Lord to transform what we love can we move to a new spiritual home.

But we are still capable of thinking more broadly: "People's thoughts spread out into the communities of spirits and angels round about them, and their ability to understand and perceive is determined by its extension into them" (AC 6599).

This teaching continues: "The extension of the thoughts and affections of people ... into different communities is what determines how much ability they have to understand and perceive" (AC 6600). Our wisdom and the goodness we are open to come from the many spiritual communities we are attached to (AC 8794:2).

Just as we know some neighborhoods near our home but not others, our thoughts and affections extend into some spiritual neighborhoods but not into others. Wiser people can stretch their minds more. That means that they know what to do in more situations they face. It means they can understand more often why the Lord acts as He does. It means they can understand and respect others more fully. It means they can more easily be around people who are different from themselves because they can see similarities and differences without feeling threatened or losing their sense of identity in the process.

By reading the Word and then applying new truths, each of us becomes a little more knowledgeable about our spiritual environment, and that expertise allows us to connect with and serve more people and to address our spiritual challenges more completely.

We Receive Goodness That Protects Us

When we are learning truths from the Word, the Lord is also accomplishing other things inside us. Once we receive truths of faith from the Word, "the Lord attaches good" (ML 128). To put it another way, the truths we know are "given life by charity and innocence" (AC 3436). We are largely unaware of this process because when we read the Word, we focus on what we are learning (ML 128). It is important to note that the goodness the Lord attaches is deeper and more powerful than mere enjoyment. The simple act of reading the Word "for the purpose of gaining wisdom" brings us in touch with levels of goodness we are rarely aware of (ML 128).

One result of the presence of goodness from within is that the Lord uses it to keep evil at bay. We are taught:

> When people who believe these [basic truths] and love the truth of them are reading the Word, everything evil and false is shifted away from them, because at that time the Lord enlightens them and leads them.... Consequently no evil at all or falsity of evil comes in, for the Lord moves them away. (AC 10638:2; AE 177:3)

The very act of reading with affection offers protection from the hells. This makes reading the Word a powerful tool for hard times. Many of us have read the Psalms when we have felt low and have been lifted up, and much of that lifting up comes from the fact that evil is being kept away. "Great peace have those who love Your law, and for them there is no stumbling" (Ps 119:165).

Reading the Word offers two kinds of protection. One is the general protection that comes from turning to the Lord and receiving His holiness into ourselves. We can use the other kind of protection during hard times, when we are being tempted, or when selfish feelings or contrarian thoughts rise up: We can actively quote and dwell on teachings from the literal meaning of Scripture. Although the negative feelings may take a while to recede, they will surely do so through the Lord's power. And as we continue to love His Word, we will find that His protection becomes more and more powerful and comprehensive.

The Angels Receive Enlightenment

One of the most commonly stated benefits of reading the Word is one we do not consciously experience: Reading the Word because we love it and want to live its truths offers enlightenment to the angels with us. When we read the Word and understand it on the natural level, they receive enlightenment and understanding on the level of the heaven they are in (AC 9152, 2176 etc.). This is a profound gift that we can offer to thousands, perhaps millions, of unseen spiritual companions as we spend daily quiet time with the Lord.

We may worry that we don't know enough to uphold the angels. But the benefit to the angels of our efforts is not based on our own deep understanding of the text. They receive a "clear perception" when we have only a "vague perception" (AC 6333:4). They receive enlightenment even when children read the Word (AC 2899, 3690:2). In fact, as we saw earlier, they have a more complete understanding when children read because of their innocent appreciation (AC 1776; SE 2435). An awareness of the benefit to angels when we read can provide comfort to us when we are struggling with sections of the Word that are hard to understand or see the relevance of. Even if we are not gaining obvious benefit ourselves, we can know that we are offering a gift to the angels.

The result of our reading and the angels' enlightenment is that heaven and earth are joined (AC 2176, 9152). In fact, this union of heaven and earth is the reason the Word has been given (AC 10452:3); without the Word, that connection would not exist (AC 9152). What is more, when angels perceive truths at a deeper level, their perception is communicated to us, giving us our light and perception (AC 8694:2). Our reading benefits the angels, which forges a connection between heaven and earth, which in turn benefits us by providing us with deeper insights.

We Offer Spiritual Nourishment to Good People

It is fairly easy to see that our reading the Word can influence the angels because of our direct connection with them. However, we may be less aware that we are also connected in spirit to the people in this world, and that reading the Word connects us to them as well. Maybe it is surprising to learn that reading also connects us to those people. The whole church on earth is like one person, and those who know the Lord and read the Word serve as the heart and lungs of that person (TCR 268). Just as the heart and lungs circulate nourishment to the body, our personal engagement with the truths of the Word spreads spiritual nourishment to those who do not have access to the Word. Think about how much the body benefits when the heart and lungs are strong and healthy. Likewise, when we read the Word and apply its truths, we enhance the quality of life for everyone in the world.

STRATEGIES FOR READING THE WORD

> *For this commandment which I command you today is not too mysterious for you, nor is it far off. It is not in heaven, that you should say, "Who will ascend into heaven and bring it to us, that we may hear it and do it?" Nor is it beyond the sea, that you should say, "Who will go over the sea for us and bring it to us, that we may hear it and do it?" But the Word is very near you, in your mouth and in your heart, that you may do it. (Deut 30:11-14)*

Many people have said that they would like to read the Word more, but they find it hard to develop a solid pattern of reading. What can we do to make it easier to overcome the obstacles that lie in the way of joyfully turning to the Word regularly? There are ways to help ourselves to make this a reality.

A first step would be to open our hearts and minds before even opening the book. We cannot turn to the Word for ideas just as we would to any other book because it requires a different level of emotional engagement from us before we can understand it. The first way to open ourselves to the Lord is to pray to Him, and we're told that those who "pray sincerely" before reading receive enlightenment from the Word (AC 5432:5, 8993:4). When we pray to the Lord, we acknowledge that in reading the Word we are "approaching the Lord alone" (Lord 2). Prayer helps us turn to the Word not as a book but as a means of conversing with the Lord. "Blessed are those who keep His testimonies, who seek Him with the whole heart" (Ps 119:2).

When we turn to the Lord directly, we enter into a dialog with Him as we read. One of the challenges with praying to the Lord is that when we talk, it can be hard to hear the Lord speaking back. That is not the case when we read. "The Lord is present and conjoined with a person through the Word because the Lord is the Word, and He, as it were, converses in it with a person" (SS 78). We can turn to the

Word with questions in our minds, and He will speak back to us. The Word has been written in a miraculous way: The Lord can give us insight into an issue or question even in a text that does not apparently relate to the issue. If we think of reading the Word as a dialogue, we open ourselves up to the natural back and forth that is supposed to happen when we read.

In order to turn to the Lord effectively in our reading, we need to treat what He says with reverence. It is not an accident that the Word has been called the Holy Bible or the Holy Book. Throughout the ages people have realized that it is holy—special in a way that nothing else is. When we treat it with that level of respect and reverence, we open ourselves up to tender feelings in our spirit, the kind that invite the Lord's presence.

"The Word is living and therefore gives life, because in its supreme sense the Lord is treated of, and in the inmost sense His kingdom, in which the Lord is all. This being the case, life itself is in the Word, life which flows into the minds of those who read the Word with reverence" (AC 3424:2). Think about holding in your hands a book that gives life because it holds life itself within it, a book that treats of the Lord, heaven, and everything that lasts. If we consider how precious such a book would be, we can see how reading it with tenderness, respect, and humility would open us to the Living Presence that is the essence of the Word.

One of the problems we face with reading the Word is that we cannot engage with the Lord in the Word unless we read with an eye to personal change. People throughout history have read for the wrong reasons: to be considered spiritual, to gain positions of power or wealth, to confirm that they were right and others were wrong, to defend evil actions, and the like (AC 3769:3, 5432:4). Reading the Word without a desire to apply what we see does little good (AC 3769:3) and in fact blinds us to the truth (AC 9382:2).

By contrast, when we read with changing our lives in mind, everything changes. Then we are approaching with the attitude expressed in this Psalm: "How can a young man cleanse his ways? By taking heed according to Your Word. With my whole heart I have inquired after You; let me not wander from Your commandments" (Ps 119:9, 10). This is what happens when we read with love for the Lord and the neighbor in mind:

> The Word is in that case opened up, for ... the whole of the Word hangs on [the law and the prophets], as does everything from them, and so everything has reference to them. And being in that case governed by the primary teachings concerning truth and good, people receive light in each particular thing they see in the Word. For the Lord is present with them at that time by means of angels and is teaching them even though they are not directly aware of it, and is also guiding them into the life of truth and good. (AC 3773)

Even if we are trying to understand something apparently abstract, such as discrete degrees or the trinity, when we read with an eye to loving the Lord and the neighbor, we will gain insight. Because of this, we are told that when we read the Word "with a view to use, such as for the sake of human society, for the sake of the Lord's Church on earth, for the sake of the Lord's kingdom in heaven, and still more for the sake of the Lord Himself ... we are opened toward Him" (AC 1472; AE 714:10). A focus on life-application in our reading changes everything.

This life-oriented approach has the capacity to cut through the snarls in our thinking that arise when we see a teaching that challenges us. If the purpose of reading is to learn to love the Lord and others, we can pause and reflect to see if we can understand the teaching, and if not, put it on a shelf for now. We can then move on, asking the Lord to show us one thing we can do based on our reading.

Focusing on what is useful leads to insight, and repeated experiences with having the Word speak to us build up confidence that the Lord is present. This confidence in turn will lead us to have a better attitude when we find other sections we do not understand or that trigger negative responses.

When we are trying to apply truth to our lives, we will naturally approach our reading with questions in mind. It can be useful to go to the Word seeking an answer to something. Having questions in mind means that we are reading with genuine curiosity. The Lord has offered us a book full of treasures. What does it hold in store for us today? In general, we retain things more when we engage with questions in mind (ML 183:2; see also Faith 71). Asking questions can be as simple as saying to the Lord in prayer, "Lord, show me one truth I need to act on today." It will make for a very different experience.

Sometimes our questions can lead us to doubt what is said. Questioning and doubting can be useful, but only insofar as they are part of a genuine search for truth. We need to love the truth for its own sake in order to find it, and we need to be looking affirmatively at what we read (AC 2568, 2588). This means we need to be looking for the spirit within the words, rather than getting fixated on particular words that bother us: "It is the spirit that gives life; the flesh profits nothing. The words that I speak to you are spirit, and they are life" (John 6:63).

The ego or proprium says, "Prove to me that this is true, and then I will believe." In reality, the ego will never believe because it will always find a way to avoid accepting. We get the most out of reading the Word if we assume that what is said there is true. It may not be true in the most obvious way. Sometimes we need to accept that the Lord means what it seems He means, and sometimes we need to discover deeper ways of understanding that teaching. How we see truth will change over time. But it will be hard to see any truth unless we are reading with the intention to affirm what is true.

While reading intentionally is important, what we read also affects us. Many people tend to read either the Heavenly Doctrines or Scripture. I would suggest that it is useful to do both and to vary our choice based on need. Reading Scripture offers a level of spiritual protection in temptation that the Heavenly Doctrines cannot (see SS 49). This is because the literal meaning of the Word is an expression of Divine truth "in its fullness, its holiness, and its power" (SS 37; TCR 111). Everyone needs that protection on a regular basis, which is why I suggest reading something from Scripture every day. When we are in the midst of a spiritual struggle, and especially when we feel like we are losing, reading Scripture can be particularly helpful.

At other times, we might emphasize reading the Heavenly Doctrines. Their explanations about the Lord, the nature of spiritual reality, the life of charity, the inner meaning of the Word, relationships, and many other truths give us perspective and peace in our lives and allow us a taste of heaven while in this world.

Read in the Context of the Doctrine of the Church

> *Those who read the Word without doctrine are like those who walk in darkness without a lamp. (AC 10582:3)*

Our final topic in this section is important enough to warrant its own heading. In order to understand the Word, we need doctrine or teaching from the church. This seems counterintuitive since we'd expect the Word to be the source of that teaching in the first place. Thus we need to explore why reading with a preexisting body of teaching in mind is so important.

Sometimes the text itself assists us when a sentence in the Word seems confusing or even shocking. If we read a little further, we may find the reason it was worded that way. The context of the words is crucial to their meaning. There are two kinds of contexts. One is the immediate context, the ideas and words that precede and follow what we are reading. For instance, the scribes and Pharisees once watched to see if the Lord would heal a man with a withered hand on the Sabbath so they could accuse Him of breaking the law. He said to them, "Is it lawful on the Sabbath to do good or to do evil, to save life or to kill?" When they kept silent, we're told that "He looked around at them with anger." The story so far presents an image of the Lord as an angry Person. Yet the full phrasing is, "He looked around at them with anger, being grieved for the hardness of their hearts" (Mark 3:1-6). Suddenly the story has a different tone, one that reflects the grief the Lord has even for those who oppose Him and wish Him to leave maimed people unhealed. His seeming anger is the outward presentation of inner sadness. Similarly, every sentence and verse in the Word needs to be seen in relation to its chapter and its broader story. At times it also needs to be seen in its historical context, including the ideas people were discussing in that era.

The second contextual tool that helps us understand confusing teachings is to look at them in the light of primary teachings. That means we can use bodies of thought to guide our understanding of particular passages. Some teachings are more important than others. For instance, one primary teaching is that the Lord is never angry with us and never punishes us (AC 245, 588); in fact, He always deals with us from mercy (AC 223). We can use these teachings to give us perspective if we read something that appears to depict the Lord as punishing or unfair. We can fall back on the general teaching that the Lord is not like that and look for a way to see the story in its true light, which is that of a loving God. Another example would be the appearance in the New Testament that Jesus is a separate being from the Father when we know from many places in the Word that there is only one God.

In the Word this body of teaching that guides our thinking as we read is called "doctrine." Surprising as this may seem, understanding the doctrine of the church comes not only as a result of our reading of the Word, but it is also an essential precursor to a proper understanding from it. Doctrine is called a lamp to those who read the Word (AC 10400; HD 257; HH 311). Without doctrine to shed light on the Word, we don't receive spiritual light (TCR 228; SS 52). We need a body of teaching to guide our thinking so we can grasp the meaning in the Word.

The Lord strongly emphasizes our need for doctrine: "The absolute truth is, that no one can understand the Word without doctrine" (AE 1089:2). And further:

> Those who read the Word without doctrine are in the dark as regards every truth. Their minds are vacillating and uncertain, prone to errors and easily led into heresies, and indeed they embrace these if they have the slightest popularity or authoritative support, and provided there is no risk to one's own reputation. (TCR 228)

The Lord gives us an image for doctrine that can help us understand its use. Doctrine is depicted in Scripture as a bow while individual truths from the Word are depicted as a sword (AE 357, 131; AC 2686). An archer can use his bow to send arrows far and wide while a swordsman's reach is more limited. The bow's wide scope suggests the broad ideas that can contain many individual truths. All the things in the Word are truths, but not all truths serve the same role. Some truths serve as doctrinal teaching, and others cannot serve as organizing principles (AE 356). For instance, the teaching that all of the Word is an expression of love for the Lord and for the neighbor is a general teaching that can be a leading doctrine. The particular truth that pride can be a form of stealing has much more limited range and cannot as easily guide our thinking as we read.

Since doctrine offers the context in which we understand truths, we can begin to understand why it is so important. Think of how differently we would read the Word if we thought that God got angry at people and cast them into hell if they misbehaved rather than that He is always loving. Or consider how profoundly important the idea is that men and women are equal partners in marriage when we read teachings about one or the other's strengths or weaknesses.

When we don't understand something we read, we can ask what general teaching would give perspective. By training ourselves to ask this question, we can start to develop doctrine from the Word for ourselves rather than relying on others.

Sometimes we can find the broader doctrine easily. At other times it can be useful to get help from people who know more than we do. One of the things that can drive us away from reading the Word is feeling that something said is unfair or unjust. It is a good idea to work through those issues as we come to them rather than letting them fester.

Even when we focus on leading doctrines, the Word is not always clear. Many thoughtful readers of the Word find things that they do not understand, sometimes things that seem wrong or that cause doubt about the truth of the Word. An important attitude to hold is that we, not the Word, are the cause of the misunderstanding (see AE 373:2). From this humble position, we can move away from putting the Word on trial, and we can constructively address the truth. We are told to affirm what we can and set aside the rest for later (AC 1072:2). This is because the things we can understand are actually few compared to the things we can't understand.

When we are attacked by doubt, another thing to remember is that "some things are obscure" to everyone reading the Word (AE 356), and that in such instances it is best to "pass them by" (AE 1180:2). When we read the Word, we need to keep in mind the general doctrines that we do understand and "not allow ourselves to be drawn away into strange doctrines by those things in the Word that do not seem to agree, and that we do not understand" (AE 356). The Lord can sort out the details in our minds over time if we hold to the general ideas we are sure of.

We may find that we cannot be open to some parts of the Word for a time. Perhaps in such instances it would be useful to consult with someone more knowledgeable. But even then we may not be able to see or to sense the love within the words. In our areas of sensitivity, we are often looking too much from the perspective of some past hurt or present concern that clouds our perception. The hurt or concern may be very real and true but carry such an emotional charge that it is best to avoid digging into that issue for a time. The Lord understands this and will lead us gradually to see how His words are loving and fair.

Read with a Long-Term View in Mind

Your Word, O Jehovah, stands to eternity in the heavens. (Ps 119:89)

The grass withers, the flower fades, but the Word of our God stands forever. (Is 40:8)

It is part of human nature to want to see the results of our efforts quickly. We know that is not always possible. We brush our teeth now so that we will have our teeth for decades, and we save now for a retirement that may seem far off.

When we read the Word, we gain benefits that we may not experience in this life. We may learn "few truths" while in the world. But within those few learned truths, we are also given many other truths related to the inner meaning of what we read, truths we will gain access to only in the next life (DP 172:5). We invest money, hoping it will grow for when we need it. If we are willing to keep investing our time and effort over the long term, reading the Word can offer a high rate of return indeed.

PRACTICAL SUGGESTIONS

When we come to the practical considerations of how to create good habits, here are some things to bear in mind: the power of ritual, of environment, and of preparation.

Rituals can be powerful, and spiritual rituals can be even more powerful. They help us find that sacred space where we can hear the Lord speaking to us. I recommend reading in the same place and at the same time whenever possible. Most people find that it works best to read at the beginning or end of the day, times when it may be easier to establish routines or habits. Those routines make it easier to get into the right frame of mind when it comes time to read.

Most people find that they read more easily in a quiet place or perhaps while listening to peaceful instrumental music. Tranquil, beautiful places cause us to lift our awareness into the higher parts of our minds and to quiet the voices of the outer world. Some people sit in a favorite chair, light a candle, or sit with a cup of their favorite tea or coffee, making reading the Word a special event.

Our minds also need some preparation as well as ritual and quiet. Sometimes we have to clear our minds before asking the Lord to fill us. When we are pressed for time and sit down to read, tense from the things we've just finished or have to do, the Lord's light may be prevented from flowing into our minds due to our other thoughts and concerns. Before reading, we might sit and breathe deeply for a few minutes and then say a prayer. Even if we have only a short time to read, we will benefit more from it if we breathe and relax first.

A PROMISE OF UNDERSTANDING

> *No longer do I call you servants, for a servant does not know what his master is doing; but I have called you friends, for all things that I heard from My Father I have made known to you. (John 15:15)*

The Word is the most holy thing we will ever hold or read. It is the source of all lasting knowledge and wisdom, and it is the means by which we can connect to the Lord and to the angels. Truth from the Word is the only vessel in our minds that can contain the Lord's love and presence. Think about reading the Word the way we think about eating. We don't live to eat, but if we don't eat, we can't live. Similarly, we don't live to read the Word, but if we don't read the Word, we cannot live the life the Lord intends for us.

We know that reading the Word is important, and we know that others have understood profound truths from the Word. But is the Lord going to give those truths to us? Angels once told some newcomers: "Read the Word and believe in the Lord, and you will see the truths which must be the truths of your faith and of your life. All in the Christian world draw their doctrinal teachings from the Word as the one only fountain.... Everyone whose soul desires it, is able to see the truths of the Word in clear light" (TCR 621:3). The Lord has made His Word accessible to us if we are willing to give our hearts to Him, perhaps not as quickly or as easily as we'd like. But He will surely reveal Himself to us and change us.

ACTIVITIES AND QUESTIONS

1. Consider embracing the challenge of reading one, two, or three pages of the Word every day. Explore what it will take to clear that time in your calendar on a regular basis.

2. Give some thought to external details that make reading the Word easier.
   a. Experiment with reading at different times to see what works for you.
   b. Journal about what holds you back from reading.
   c. Make a space in your home that is your Word-reading area.
   d. Some people like to keep a journal with them so they can write down the verses or phrases they like or the ideas that come to them as they read.

   e. Are there rituals you can develop that would make it easier to get into the state of mind that supports worship?

3. Even on days when you are too tired, consider reading or reciting at least one verse from Scripture.

4. Try reading with application in mind. Before you begin, pray that the Lord will show you one thing that can guide your life today.

5. Imagine your reading as a gift to the angels and to all in the world who benefit from having the Word read.

Make Time for Reflection

Mary kept all these sayings and pondered them in her heart.
(Luke 2:19)

We have already touched on the topic of reflection many times because it is not possible to do any of the things we have explored so far without reflection. But because it is so important, and because the Lord mentions it as a regular daily practice, I offer here some teachings about reflection as a tool and support to our spiritual lives.

Broadly speaking, reflection is an ability of our inner self to rise above our lower concerns and to consider what they are. Reflection gives us the perspective to see if something is true and what we are really like. It is an ability that can be developed and strengthened through supporting practices.

As we practice, we gain self-awareness, which is at the heart of our capacity to change rather than to simply act on what we feel (SE 2838, 2845). When we see things, we can change them. As we saw earlier, "What people know nothing about is unintelligible to them even if it happens to them" (AC 5365:3, 5649:3). And further, once something becomes familiar or habitual, we do not reflect on it (SE 3605, 3050-51). These teachings show why it is hard to change bad habits and also why we can sometimes drift away from good habits without noticing.

Over and over in the Word we are told to pay attention. "Listen and hear my voice; pay attention and hear my speech" (Is 28:23). "What I say to you, I say to all: Watch!" (Mark 13:37). If reflection is anything, it is paying attention and noticing what is actually happening (AC 4906, 8514; D Love 18:4). In particular, it is noticing what the Lord teaches and paying attention to what He values. The benefit of reflection is that it leads us to pay attention to the truly important things rather than the most pressing or seemingly urgent ones. Each of the following sections describes a different way to learn to pay better attention and so to reflect more fully.

A kind of paying attention that is popular today is the meditation that is practiced in many parts of Asia, largely as an expression of Buddhist, Hindu, or Daoist principles. I will refer to ways in which the practices of meditation described in the Word can be supported by the meditation practices of these faiths.

MINDFULNESS: REMEMBERING AND FORGETTING

What is man that You are mindful of him, and the son of man that You visit him?" (Ps 8:4)

What the Lord is Scripture refers to as "remembering" is often called "mindfulness" today. This is the goal of spiritual living: to become mindful of the Lord even when we are doing other things. We know the Lord is always present, but we turn our attention to Him only occasionally; it is as if we remember that He exists only at those times.

Time and again the Lord tells the Israelites that they are forgetting Him: "Therefore thus says the Lord Jehovih: 'Because you have forgotten Me and cast Me behind your back, therefore you shall bear your crimes and your harlotry'" (Ezek 23:35; see also Jud 3:7; 1 Sam 12:9). And in other places the Lord emphasizes that we need to remember Him: "And you shall remember Jehovah your God, for it is He who gives you power to get wealth, that He may establish His covenant which He promised to your fathers, as it is this day" (Deut 8:18; see Ex 13:3; Ps 20:7).

We pay attention to and remember what is important to us:

As regards faith, when we receive and possess faith we are constantly mindful of the Lord. This is so even when we are thinking or talking about something other than Him, or else when we are carrying out our public, private, or family duties, though we are not directly conscious of our mindfulness of the Lord while carrying them out. Indeed that mindfulness of the Lord present in those who possess faith governs their whole being, but ... is not noticed by them except when they turn their thought specifically to that matter. (AC 5130)

The ultimate mindfulness comes when we develop a living awareness of the Lord:

It should be recognized that all evil flows in from hell and all good from the Lord by way of heaven.... [I]f we believed what is really so, we would think, the instant evil flowed in, that it came from the evil spirits present with us; and since that was what we thought, the angels would ward that evil off and repel it. (AC 6206; AC 6324)

This level of mindfulness is highly spiritual. Most of us achieve it only occasionally.

Despite our lack of awareness, the Lord is always mindful of us, every moment of every day. "He has given food to those who fear Him; He will ever be mindful of His covenant" (Ps 111:5). "The Lord has been mindful of us; He will bless us" (Ps 115:12). As we choose to become more mindful of Him in return, we gain peace and safety, and this is our greatest blessing.

Reflection (mindfulness) involves our learning to pay attention to the important things by regularly calling them to mind in our daily lives, just as the Lord constantly gives us His attention and love. This is why so many of the techniques for meditation encourage us to pay attention to one thing, such as our breathing. When we learn to focus or concentrate, we cultivate the ability to reflect on spiritual matters by paying particular attention to them.

To pay proper attention, we need to consciously move into our inner self. Only what is internal in us can reflect: "Nothing can look into itself; but it must be something more internal or higher that thinks about it, for this can look into it" (AC 1953). It is as if we need to lift our minds to a higher elevation to get perspective on our thoughts and emotions, similar to climbing a hill or a tower to view the terrain. "When the mind is elevated, attention is awakened" (AE 263). Unless we do this, we are like the fish that cannot observe the water it is swimming in.

Reflection and meditation require us to put aside the cares of the world and lift our attention above them for a time to gain perspective. This is why people who want to reflect about life normally go off to a quiet place where they are able to rise above worldly concerns.

STOPPING

> *Be still and know that I am God. (Ps 46:10)*
>
> *Busyness is the enemy of spirituality. It is essentially laziness. It is doing the easy thing instead of the hard thing. It is filling our time with our own actions instead of paying attention to God's actions.*[1]

Reflection is lifting up our minds to pay attention to the Lord and to what is real. A necessary first step is to clear our minds to do this. Reflection requires that we stop doing other things—stop being busy—to create the space for reflection to take place. Reflection is "a seeing of past events, hence, recognition of oneself" (SE 2107). In fact, the word "reflect" means to turn back or turn around in the sense of looking back at our past to consider our character or looking back at things in our memory to consider their nature.

Seeing past events, or "turning back," involves stopping (see AC 8514); we do not walk forward while looking back. We saw earlier that people who are busy with making a living sometimes do not have the time or ability to reflect about spiritual matters (SS 59; TCR 354:3). The ability to stop—to take a Sabbath rest—is required

---

[1]Eugene Peterson, *Subversive Spirituality* Grand (Rapids, MI: William B. Eerdmans Publishing Company, 1997) 237.

(TCR 301). Perhaps this is why "meditating on things related to salvation and eternal life" is one of the ways of remembering the Sabbath (TCR 301; AE 54).

When we say we are too busy, we are usually not seeing clearly. We make time for what we value, even time-consuming and challenging activities. What we are really saying is that in the press of daily living, spiritual disciplines seem less important than getting through the day. While that may be true at times, if it is the pattern of our life, we may need to rethink how we are living.

Perhaps, then, we need to reframe what stopping means. For instance, during busy times in our lives, we may find that reading the Word every day is hard to do or that we read just a few verses at the end of the day. That's fine. The Lord understands our situation and appreciates our effort to turn to Him as much as we can. Spiritually speaking, our challenge is to value reading the Word, prayer, repentance, and serving others as much as we do eating and sleeping, to see these as vital activities that we build our other activities around, at least over the broad sweep of months and years. Over time we need to give ourselves permission to let what is important be important. We can sometimes become so driven by pressing earthly matters that we don't allow ourselves to do what our best self wants to do. It can be a blessed relief to allow ourselves to stop doing what is urgent in the short term and to focus instead on what is important for the long term.

What are the enemies of stopping and mindfulness? Stopping can be a bigger challenge than it seems because it means we have to confront the powerful and seductive emotion of anxiety. Anxiety may be the common underlying emotion in consumerist Western society. Advertising caters to our fears; newspapers and websites herald the latest disaster or disease and proclaim outrage over various issues; time-driven deadlines and goal-driven performance reviews dominate work life; and magazines, websites, and our inner fears can push us to measure up to the notions of what a perfect relationship should look like. It is easy to feel that disaster is looming and that by working harder and longer we might avert it.

In essence, anxiety arises from being deprived of the things we love (AC 2689). Because our natural self is drawn to many worldly loves, we can easily find ourselves anxious about losing many material and selfish things. "Anxiety comes chiefly from [anxious spirits with us] being of such a nature that they keep their thoughts fixed on the one subject, and do not dispel anxious feelings by variety.... In this way they keep another's lower mind fixed on certain thoughts" (AC 5391). Anxiety also drives us to worry about future events which all too often means we are taking on the management of life events that belongs only to the Lord (AC 5177). Both these—fixating on certain ideas and worrying about the future—pull us down and away from spiritual life. And once they are active in us they don't stop, since "there are never wanting things to strengthen doubt and make it burdensome" (AC 5386).

When evil spirits hold us for long enough in anxious thoughts, we can become depressed, further limiting meaningful reflection (SE 3624, 3625). Anxiety, then, is a central enemy to stopping and to reflection.

By contrast, angels are not anxious about the future. They call anxiety "care for the morrow, which they define as grief on account of losing or not receiving things that are not necessary for the uses of life" (HH 278:2). Our anxieties lead us to lose a sense of proportion, placing too much value on what is not important or on what we cannot control.

Because angels keep perspective, they are able to trust the Lord, knowing that He always leads to a good end. We on earth do the same to the extent that we are in the stream of Providence (AC 8478:3). Anxiety tends to tell us that we have to strive really hard or disaster will befall us, or that no matter what we do, disaster will occur. Trusting in the Lord reminds us that we certainly have to do our part, but the Lord does the real work. We can rest in the thought that because His power in infinite, He is able to overcome in all areas of spiritual life.

Saying No

> *Thus says the Lord Jehovih, the Holy One of Israel: "In returning to Me and rest you shall be saved; in quietness and trust shall be your strength." (Is 30:15)*

In order to say yes to what is most important, we often need to say no to distractions and sometimes even to other good things. We need to say no to the pressing concerns that prevent us from reflecting, or to put it another way, to the anxious spirits who want to keep us from elevating our minds so we can reflect. Only when we say no to the external things that consume our attention can we make appropriate choices about our lives at a deeper level.

These anxious spirits often act on us by making us aware of the many things that bombard us from the outside—chores, tasks, people we need to see and please. These things are good and important, but none are as important as our spiritual life. Being able to reflect means placing a high priority on the quiet time that reflection requires and saying no to issues that are less important.

Stephen Covey shares a story that is a deeper dive into saying no. He explains how saying no is a precursor to being able to say yes to what is most important.

I attended a seminar once where the instructor was lecturing on time. At one point, he said, "Okay, it's time for a quiz." He reached under the table and pulled out a wide-mouth gallon jar. He set it on the table next to a platter with some fist-sized rocks on it. "How many of these rocks do you think we can get in the jar?" he asked.

After we made our guess, he said, "Okay. Let's find out." He set one rock in the jar ... then another ... then another. I don't remember how many he got in, but he got the jar full. Then he asked, "Is the jar full?"

Everybody looked at the rocks and said, "Yes."

Then he said, "Ahhh." He reached under the table and pulled out a bucket of gravel. Then he dumped some gravel in and shook the jar and the gravel went in all the little spaces left by the big rocks. Then he grinned and said once more, "Is the jar full?"

By this time we were on to him. "Probably not," we said.

"Good!" he replied. And he reached under the table and brought out a bucket of sand. He started dumping the sand in and it went in all the little spaces left by the big rocks and the gravel. Once more he looked at us and said, "Is the jar full?"

"No!" we all roared.

He said, "Good!" and he grabbed a pitcher of water and began to pour it in. He got something like a quart of water in that jar. Then he said, "Well, what's the point?"

Somebody said, "Well, there are gaps, and if you really work at it, you can always fit more into your life."

"No," he said, "that's not the point. The point is this: if you hadn't put these big rocks in first, would you ever have gotten any of them in?"[1]

Our spiritual life in definitely a big rock. But for many of us, thinking about our spiritual life fits in after we've done our work, taken care of the chores, spent time with friends, exercised, caught up on social media, and had some down time. Saying no often means scheduling quiet time first or putting it at the top of our list of things to do when free time occurs. The Lord says the same thing about the order in which we should do things:

> Therefore do not worry, saying, 'What shall we eat?' or 'What shall we drink?' or 'What shall we wear?' For after all these things the Gentiles seek. For your heavenly Father knows that you need all these things. But seek first the kingdom of God and His justice, and all these things shall be added to you." (Matt 6:31-33)

One way to put our spiritual life first is to make it part of the morning or bedtime ritual, or possibly our post-dinner or lunch-break ritual. We have to create times that are long enough that we are not anxiously thinking about the next event, and our minds can rise up, free of natural concerns.

Doing this involves discipline and mental focus. We need to build up our mental strength and stamina so we can block out concerns that pull our minds down in

---

[1]Stephen Covey, A. Roger Merrill, and Rebecca Merrill, *First Things First* (New York: Simon & Schuster, 1994), 88-89.

the quiet moments. For example, if we decide to get up half an hour early to say prayers, read the Word, and reflect, but during that time we are worrying about the upcoming day, that half hour will not have been spent in meaningful reflection. The mental discipline of sending away anxious spirits is vital to our success.

Think for a moment of the freedom that comes from putting important things first, the ease of mind from living our ideals, the joy of expressing what is most important to us, the peace that comes from stopping in a busy world to be present with the Lord. Spiritual practices give us all these gifts.

The first steps of saying no, then, are to decide what are most important in our lives and then to build the rest of our lives around those values. Doing so requires that we say no to other things, things that can be good but that are less important. By creating space for the most important things, we give ourselves breathing room to think from what we value rather than having what is urgent dictate what we think about. Taking these steps allow us the emotional space in which to move on to the next step of saying no, which is to say no to deeper hellish desires.

Swedenborg observed how focusing too much on worldly matters affected him:

> Whenever I have been considering some heavenly idea and have then lapsed into thoughts about worldly and earthly matters, heavenly things have faded so much from view that they could barely be recognized. The reason for this is that what belongs to the superior light of heaven turns into darkness when it sinks to the level of what belongs to the inferior light of the world. (AC 6309:2)

If we are trying to read the Word or pray but are anxious about how much time we have, that worldly concern will pull our minds away from really paying attention to the spiritual message the Lord is giving us. It is the same if we are worried about finances, tasks to be done, relationships, and the like. Perhaps this is why many regular readers of the Word find that reading first thing in the morning works best; they carve out a time before the cares of the world have welled up so they can give their full attention to the text.

The way we build this protected space will not be the same as the way we create a space for, say, exercise, which can be done when the mind is full of other thoughts. Although we live in a world in which people consider it normal to listen to music and check social media in the middle of a project, spiritual practice does not lend itself to multitasking. Swedenborg's experience illustrates how thoughts we dwell on cause us trouble:

> Any objects of thoughts which, when one is held in them, or one's reflection is kept fixed upon them by spirits, create a great deal of trouble—for the most part having to do with one's own affairs, or things that are to come, as is evident from much experience. Whenever I was prompted to think of my little garden, of him who cared for it, of my having to be called home, of money matters, of the attitude

of my acquaintances, of the character of the people in my house, of things that were to be written, how they would be received by the people and the possibility that they would not be understood, of new clothes that had to be obtained, and many other such cares—whenever I was kept reflecting on them for a long time, spirits would straightway throw in troublesome, worrisome, and evil things, together with supporting thoughts and desires. (SE 3624)

Spiritual living requires that we intentionally say no to many good things so that we can say yes to more important ones. It requires that we plan our time, and it requires that we push away distracting thoughts in the moment when they come in. When we do these things, our minds can rise up to a higher level from which we can reflect with insight about what we need to do in our lives.

LIVING IN THE PRESENT

> *This is the day that Jehovah has made. We will rejoice and be glad in it. (Ps 118:24)*

> *The present moment is filled with joy and happiness. If you are attentive, you will see it. (Thích Nhat Hanh)*[1]

In order to pay attention and reflect, we have to stop living in the past or the future. Instead, we need to pay attention to the present day that the Lord has made for us. Spiritual living takes place when we are experiencing and thinking about what is happening now yet with the past and future in mind. Natural living leads us to live *for* the present without considering the future (see AE 1165), to live in the future (such as when we worry about getting things done or are afraid of the outcomes of our actions, of what people will think, or about the state of the world), or to live in the past (such as when we are driven by guilt, regret, or trauma to act in certain ways, or when we long for days gone by in a way that makes us discontent with the present). In all these circumstances, our minds stay in the external part of ourselves or at best pop briefly into awareness of our inner self. In order to live spiritually, we need to find ways to remain mindfully in the present moment. This requires a reflective awareness of our thoughts and feelings that is not easy to come by.

Living in the present is important. For the Lord and the angels, everything is present: "With the Lord, and consequently in the angelic heaven, the future and the present are one and the same, for what is future is already present, or what is

---

[1]Thích Nhat Hanh, *Peace Is Every Step: The Path of Mindfulness in Everyday Life* (New York: Bantam Books, 1991), 21.

to take place has taken place"[1] (AC 730:5, 2788, 9787). By contrast, people on earth cannot help but think in terms of time and space (AC 3404). Thinking from time and space makes it easy to get caught up in the past or future, while angels, for whom the present includes the past and the future, have no anxiety about the future (AC 1382).

A beautiful teaching shows us what living in the present is actually like:

> I have spoken to angels about the memory of things of the past and about consequent anxiety concerning things of the future, and I have been informed that the more interior and perfect angels are, the less do they care about things of the past or think about those of the future, and that this is also the origin of their happiness. They have said that the Lord provides them every moment with what to think, accompanied by blessing and happiness, and that this being so they have no cares and no worries. This also is what is meant in the internal sense by the manna being received "day by day" from heaven, and by the "daily [provision] of bread" in the Lord's Prayer, as well as by the statement that they must not worry about what they are to eat and drink, or what clothes they are to put on. But although angels have no care about things of the past and are not worried about those of the future, they nevertheless have a most perfect recollection of things of the past and a most perfect insight into those of the future, because their entire present includes both the past and future within it. (AC 2493)

Angels appear to have achieved that "Zen" space of tranquillity, trusting in the Lord's care. Because they are aware of the Lord's providence, they are willing to be open to what is, confident that they will be able to discern and choose what is needed. We cannot yet be angels, but we can experience some of that trust and peace. We know that in those angelic states of mind, it is much easier to reflect in the moment on what is needed and to react appropriately. It's as if time slows down, and we have all the time we need to make decisions with integrity and peace.

We human beings rarely experience the effortless wisdom of the angels, but we can approach it:

> When we enter a state of love or heavenly affection, we enter an angelic state; that is to say, it is as though time does not exist, provided that that affection holds no urge for change.... When we experience these, we are not conscious of time, since we are living within the internal self during such experiences. By means of the affection that is an attribute of genuine love we are drawn away from bodily and

---

[1] This passage is particularly valuable in thinking about living in the present because this statement comes in the middle of a section on temptation. The Lord is not saying that if we live in the present, all our troubles will disappear. He is saying that if we live in the present with integrity, He will be with us and will guide us in overcoming whatever trials beset us.

worldly interests, for our minds are lifted up towards heaven, and so we are drawn away from things that belong to time. (AC 3827)

We can experience a heavenly sense of timelessness when we allow heavenly affections to guide us and when we are able to do so apart from any sense of urgency or anxiety. We can experience a lesser form of it when we are caught up in doing or talking about something we love. Internal affections are always timeless. Living in the present, in the sense of living in the Lord's presence right now, inherently opens us up to heavenly states and so to reflection. So one way we can learn to live in the present is to focus on living our lives from heavenly affection.

Living in the present does not mean that we do not plan for the future or reflect on the past. These are important and necessary things to do. As the passage said about angels, "Their entire present includes both the past and future within it" (AC 2493). Most of us have experienced being so worried about some future event that we have completely forgotten an important current event, and then regretted that absence later. That is acting from anxiety. Living in the present requires that we remember that the Lord is with us and powerful even as we pay attention to the future concerns that we need to provide for and as we reflect on our past actions.

When we live in the present, we become attuned to reality, the reality of the Lord's presence here and now. Living in the present is not simply a technique for lessening anxiety and regret; it is an assertion that our focus on the past and the future engages us in false realities. And it allows us to be compassionately present to the pain around us and in us in a way that brings the Lord's healing. We can deal with the past and the future from the present and in the present. But living in the past or for the future, or thinking excessively about the past or the future, means we are living in an illusion. Spiritual living takes place in the present.

There is a lot of literature about mindfulness and living in the present. Perhaps the most famous is the work of Thích Nhat Hanh, a Buddhist monk.[1] Mindfulness is the effort to live intentionally, to radically monotask in a multitask world. Do one thing, and give it your full attention. Many Buddhists would say that the meditation techniques they teach are merely "practice living," meaning that they teach us to become present in the moment so that when we go through ordinary life we can do so mindfully and reflectively.[2] This may be the most useful of the Asian meditation ideas because it offers a way to be reflective in a way that leads to activity and usefulness. The point of any reflection or meditation is not to become the guru on

---

[1] *The Miracle of Mindfulness* is his seminal work, but he has written many others, approaching mindfulness from Buddhist principles that work well with New Church teaching.

[2] Ezra Bayda, *Being Zen: Bringing Meditation to Life* (Boston: Shambala, 2003), 11.

the mountaintop, removed from the world; it is to become an active and useful citizen of the world (see ML 1-10).

Breathing: Harmonizing Internal and External Activity

Jehovah is in His holy temple. Let all the earth keep silence before Him.
(Hab 2:20)

The meditation technique of becoming aware of our breathing is a powerful way to learn to live in the present.[1] Perhaps more than anything else, meditation is about limiting the chatter of earthly concerns so that we can become aware of a deeper reality. Meditation teachers say that sitting in an upright relaxed position, breathing deeply, and focusing on a word or object or one's breathing to the exclusion of other things allows us to calm our natural mind so that it comes into harmony with our deeper spirit.

One passage strongly points out the need for harmony between our spirit and body, particularly with regard to our breath:

> We cannot think at all without the concurrence and support of the breath of our lungs. So quiet thought is accompanied by quiet breathing, deep thought by deep breathing. We hold and release our breath, we suppress or intensify our breathing, in response to our thinking—in response, then, to the inflow of some feeling related to what we love, breathing slowly, rapidly, eagerly, gently, or intently. In fact, if we suppress our breathing completely, we cannot think except in our spirit, by its breathing, which is not clearly noticeable. (DLW 382)

In general, the teaching is that our mental state affects our breathing, rather than the other way around (see SE 3320, 3464), and our bodily awareness fades as we focus deeply on spiritual matters (AC 6313, 4413, 5141). This makes sense in that our spirit directs our everyday life, and the body follows suit. At the same time, what we do with our body can aid our spirit in finding a new state. We have all experienced taking a few calming breaths to enable us to think rationally after a shock, so we know it works the other way around too. Even then, it is our minds that choose those slow breaths to help another part of the mind to slow down. Most meditation techniques involve focusing on breathing, and given the correspondence of breath with thinking, this makes sense. When we discipline our minds enough to calm our breathing, the deeper awareness and activity of our spirit can become perceptible to us.

---

[1] In this section I am offering a spiritual perspective that might aid the reader in benefiting from the many breathing techniques that are taught today.

However, breathing deeply does not lead to spiritual insight. We should not confuse technique with result. Most meditation breathing techniques spring from the assumption that if we can clear the mind of natural concerns, we will enter a pure and peaceful state of being. While we will likely find natural peace doing this, spiritual peace requires more work. If we breathe deeply and with relaxation, we will create the external space within which we can then read the Word or pray or reflect without the distraction of natural concerns. Spiritual work involves overt spiritual activities in addition to the willingness to rest in the Lord's presence.

Here is one way to think about making the practice of mindful breathing a more overtly spiritual one. We read in Genesis, "And Jehovah God formed man of the dust of the ground, and breathed into his nostrils the breath of life; and man became a living being" (Gen 2:7). We could think of this as merely a metaphorical description of creation. But we could also see it as a real description of how the Lord breathes life into us every moment and how the breathing we do is both a real and metaphorical reception of the Lord's life (see AC 94-97). If we then remind ourselves of the quote, "Jehovah is in His holy temple. Let all the earth keep silence before Him" (Hab 2:20), we can invite the Lord into the temple of our mind with each breath and seek to have all other things be silent before Him, breathing out what is not the Lord's in us. An approach such as this could make a meditation technique a more spiritual experience.

PULLING IT TOGETHER

Life can feel like we do what we have to so we can eventually do what we want to. This means that life can feel a bit out of our control. Looking deeper shows that we can make choices; we can redirect our lives and develop non-negotiable guidelines that over time become what we want in our lives. To accomplish this, we need to find ways to stop busyness and hold anxiety at bay so that in the present moment we can devote time to the Lord and His ways.

There are many techniques that can help us with mindfulness. We can use those techniques in the light of the Lord's teaching to bring us into the present moment, free of anxiety. As we still our minds and learn to contain the affections that drive us, we find that the Lord is already present with us. In the light of His presence, we will be able to reflect on what is most important and make good decisions.

The peace that comes from reflectively stopping is a gift beyond measure, and it requires firm boundaries on our part to make it happen. Each of us will create that space differently, and what we choose to make time and emotional space for will determine the kind of person we become. Over our lifetime we will learn to carve out better and better spaces for Him, step by step.

ACTIVITIES AND QUESTIONS

1. Does your daily life reflect your values as much as you would like?
   a. What are the "big rock" activities you want to build into your schedule?
   b. Consider making a daily or weekly schedule that puts the spiritual big rock elements in first and then builds the rest of your life around them.
   c. What would you have to consider giving up to make room for the big rocks?
   d. What would you like to gain from doing this?

2. Reflection is paying attention.
   a. What would you like to pay more attention to?
   b. What would you like to pay less attention to?

3. Reflection is moving inward toward the Lord.
   a. What is one thing that drags you down into worldly concerns that you could work on limiting in your life?
   b. What practices and thoughts bring you into a mental state that allows you to think about the Lord and His values?

4. Reflection is stopping.
   a. What might you need to stop doing so that you have more time and emotional space to reflect?
   b. What are some anxieties that lead you to block out the Lord's presence in your life?

5. Reflection requires living in the present.
   a. What would living in the present look like for you?
   b. What fear or anxiety or grief or anger or shame would you need to face and address so you can live in the present?
   c. Consider stopping right now and breathing quietly for five minutes. What do you notice?
   d. What do you think the Lord would like you to do at this very moment?

As Much Healing and
Peace As We Want

These things I have spoken to you, that in Me you may have peace.
(John 16:33)

We know the Lord expects us to develop gradually, taking on one thing at a time, but the gap between where we are and where we think we should be can feel large. All these teachings about spiritual practice taken together can feel overwhelming the way the thought of running a marathon might overwhelm an unfit person. The Lord offers us a full program if we want to rise toward becoming all that He has in mind for us. It is important to note that each stage along the way has its joys. Our practices will slowly open our hearts so we can feel more joy and peace, but the whole journey is good. If we start the journey, the Lord will take us, step by step, through the levels of engagement, as far as we want to go, bringing us greater joy at each step.

The Living Waters of the Word

We might wonder what steps of development we can expect to go through as we apply these spiritual practices. The Lord gave Ezekiel a vision that describes the gradual progress we can make over the course of our lives as we engage is spiritual living. The vision describes what the land would look like when the Messiah came, and in its inner meaning it describes what our lives can look like depending on how much we let the Lord in. In the vision, a river issues from the altar in the temple at the center of the land, flowing east.

> When the man went out eastward, with a line in his hand, he measured a thousand cubits, and he made me cross through in the waters; the waters were to the ankles. And he measured a thousand, and made me pass through the waters; the waters were to the knees. And he measured a thousand, and made me pass through; the waters were to the loins. And he measured a thousand, and it was a river that I was not able to pass through; for the waters were risen up, waters of swimming, a river that he did not pass through. And he said to me, "Son of man, have you seen this?"... Now when I had returned, behold, at the bank of the river were very many trees on the one side and on the other. And he said to me, "These waters went out toward the east boundary, and go down into the desert, and come toward the sea. They are brought to the sea, and the waters shall be healed. And it shall be that every living soul which crawls, wherever the rivers come, will live.

There will be very many fish, because these waters come there; for they shall be healed; and everything shall live wherever the river comes. And it shall be that the fishermen shall stand on it from En Gedi to En Eglaim; they will be a place for spreading nets. Their fish shall be according to their kinds, as the fish of the Great Sea, exceedingly many. But the swamps and the marshes will not be healed; they shall be given over to salt.

And by the river upon its bank, on this side and on that, shall come up all trees for food, whose leaf shall not fade, and whose fruit shall not be finished; it shall renew its fruits every month, because its waters went out from the sanctuary. And their fruit shall be for food, and its leaf for healing. (Ez 47:1-12)

In the prior chapter, the Lord gives a detailed vision of the temple that would be built. The temple is a symbol for our willingness to make the Lord and His will central to our lives, which is what the practices we have been exploring lead us to do. From that temple flows a river—His truth—that heals us.

When an angel measures 1000-cubit (1500-foot) increments, the water is at first ankle deep, then knee deep, then up to the loins or waist, then over the head. These four measurements describe four levels of commitment we can make to following the Lord. Each of them is a point at which it becomes harder to resist the flow of the river, a point at which we become more willing to act from the Lord and His truth. We might think of them as describing the levels of devotion we can have to the practices of following the Lord.

Ankle-Deep Engagement

When we are willing to engage with the Lord's truth up to our ankles we are dabbling in the truth: We are letting it touch us only a bit. Ankle-deep engagement in these spiritual practices might be reading the Word or going to church because it is interesting, because we like to know facts, or because we want to get ahead but don't want to change the way we live. Ankle-deep engagement might be thinking seriously about truth when we go to church but not giving it much thought at any other time. Ankle-deep engagement might be thinking we are fine because we were raised in the New Church when we have not actually applied that truth when it was inconvenient. Ankle-deep engagement might be deciding we are good because we are generous even though we do not intentionally turn away from what is wrong or do good because it is the Lord's will.

Knee-Deep Engagement

When we wade knee-deep in the Lord's truth, we have made a commitment to follow the Lord though it is not yet a strong commitment. Even though we want to be affected by Him, we want to preserve the option to reject His way. When we are knee-deep in water, we can lift our legs out of the water and move in any direction with relative ease.

This represents the lowest level of heaven—the natural heaven. When water comes up to our knees, spiritually, we obey truth when we are told, and we will even make some effort to find it, but we are tempted to lift our feet free of the healing waters at times. We like being a good person, but we want to be our own person. We tell the truth, but there are times when we may stretch it. We love marriage, but we may laugh at dirty jokes. Doing the spiritual practices at this level may feel like hard work because we are more focused on obeying the rules ("You should read the Word every day," "Go to church every Sunday") than on entering into the deeper spirit of those rules. Even though we may not get the enjoyment from them that we would like, the practices will benefit us a great deal.

Waist-Deep Engagement

When we engage up to the waist, or loins, we are permanently in the water. If we want to fight the direction of the stream, we have to work hard. This represents the commitment of the angels of the middle heaven. They are committed to truth; they seek it out. They may resist hard truths for a time, but fundamentally they are willing, even eager, to obey the Lord's truth.

When we are in up to our waist, we can resist the current when it is not strong, but must move with it when it is strong. Spiritual angels may want to stop to think about truth when it is not critical, but when the Lord's truth is clear, they obey it willingly. When we reach this level of commitment to spiritual practice, we start to relish the time we set aside for the Lord each day, and we find that we build our day around these practices rather than fitting in the practices around the rest of our activities. We still struggle to do what we know we should, but in general we fight hard to make the Lord's will a priority.

Total Engagement

When we enter water that is over our heads, we can be afraid. This section describes what it feels like to give our lives fully to the Lord. The selfish part of us that wants to be in charge feels like we are about to drown, like we are giving up free will. In an era when most people could not swim, this is undoubtedly how many ancient Israelites would have felt about entering deep water. It is frightening to trust that the Lord's way will truly save us. It appears at times that it will not, that it will kill our enjoyment of life.

To the good part of us, entering water over our heads feels like we are being set free from worry and control over our lives. Few are willing to take this risk of trusting in the Lord, of moving at His direction. When we do this, we develop a trust similar to the celestial angels' trust in the Lord. We allow ourselves to float in the stream of His leading. This is what the Lord was telling us to do when He told Peter to forgive seventy times seven times (Matt 18:22): Don't keep count with people; give up the right to judge someone as altogether evil; give up the right to hate. Going in over our heads means that when we hear a truth, we do not debate within ourselves about whether we should obey it; we simply start planning how to obey it. This is floating along in the stream of providence.

We are engaged in these spiritual practices at this level when they become part of the fabric of our lives. We turn to the Lord regularly in the day because how else would one live life? We go to church on Sunday because we have trouble imagining doing anything else. Reading the Word and prayer are times of solace and peace in our busy days.

Healing What Can Be Healed

The river in the vision flows into the Dead Sea, which is the lowest point on earth. Water plunges down steep cliffs that have no outlet. Because it is in such a hot area, the water evaporates, leaving behind its minerals. Over time, the Dead Sea has become so salty that nothing can live in it. This is what lives controlled by evil can look like. An angry person, or a deceitful person, or someone prone to gossip, can fall into this vicious cycle in which all the goodness and truth in a situation is ignored and the evil remains. They may want a solution to the deadness but feel trapped by the poisonous cycle.

In Ezekiel's vision, when the river flowed into the Dead Sea, the impossible happened: The waters were healed. The water pouring down into the Dead Sea is like truth pouring into wounded parts of our lives and healing them. We could also think of the healing power of water washing out a wound so it can heal. No natural water could heal the Dead Sea, so this healing is a miracle of the Lord's presence. This is the reason for the spiritual practices presented in this book: They invite the Lord's presence to allow for miraculous healing that is not otherwise possible.

The story also says that the swamps and marshes are not healed but are given over to salt. Parts of us cannot be healed; they serve no useful function, and the Lord allows them to die. Painful memories of wicked things we have done need to fade away. Subtle pride that destroys our desire to worship or to humble ourselves before the Lord needs to die. Belligerent attitudes that refuse to accept any truth but what we come up with need to die. These deaths are as merciful as the healing. Regrets and old pains can destroy our ability to feel the Lord's joy in the moment. He wants us to let them die as we focus on His will in the here and now.

As Much Healing and Peace As We Want

If we are willing to walk the path He has set before us, the Lord offers us a complete healing of our spirits. He knows that even if we want that healing, it can happen only gradually as we move deeper and deeper into the stream of His providence. As we do this, we experience abundant goodness, just as in Ezekiel's story fruit trees bore fruit every month, and people caught fish of every kind from what was once the Dead Sea.

Receiving those blessings requires trusting that the Lord's way will bring peace. He tells us, "Peace I leave with You, my peace I give to you; not as the world gives, do I give to you. Let not your heart be troubled. Neither let it be afraid" (John 14:27).

WHAT MIGHT A FULL PROGRAM LOOK LIKE?

Applying all the spiritual practices in this book might feel daunting and time consuming. But the Lord does not expect something unreasonable from us. Here is an attempt to offer a program for daily, weekly, and more occasional activity, organized around the two great commandments of loving the Lord and loving the neighbor.

Daily Activity

We turn to the Lord each day by reading the Word, several pages or several chapters; by praying morning, evening, and at meals; and by taking an inventory of how we did with moral living that day (daily repentance or reflection). When we are busy or just starting out, we might read only a few verses every day and say a prayer.

We serve our neighbor each day by justly and faithfully working at our primary occupation. A good starting point might be to ask the Lord to show us one way we could do our daily job a bit better.

Weekly Activity

Each week we turn to the Lord by attending church, in person if possible, and by spending some time in more meaningful reflection about our life and the Lord's Word, perhaps as part of our Sabbath. When particularly busy or starting out, we might feel that we cannot always make the time to attend church. When that is not possible, a few minutes of prayer and reflection could give us a Sabbath rest.

Each week we love the neighbor by serving others as an act of kindness. Perhaps we could do this as part of our Sabbath practice. We would also attend to our duties (paying taxes, caring for family, paying bills, and such) and make time for recreation so we will be able to serve others with energy and focus. In busy times we might want to skip these practices, but doing so will have consequences if we do that too often.

Issues to Work on from Time to Time

We turn to the Lord by giving attention to our idea of Him, making sure we have a clear concept of a visible God and thinking about His qualities. Christmas and Easter might be good times to do this, or perhaps at New Year and New Church Day. We also turn to the Lord when we actively seek to discover and then shun the dominant evil in our life. This is a way of serving our neighbor as well. And finally, we turn to the Lord when we take Holy Supper several times a year.

We serve our neighbor in another way by taking a meaningful vacation to refresh ourselves in order to serve them better.

Our job is to choose one or two of these practices and start to integrate them into our lives. Then add another and another. And then notice the miracle of the Lord's transformation as we make His will the center of our lives.

How Much Time Does This Take?

The Lord is asking for surprisingly little time from us. Here is an attempt at quantifying the commitment that spiritual living takes. The numbers are suggestions designed to point out that we can be actively spiritual without making huge adjustments to our already busy schedules.

As we progress in these practices, we may find that we want to spend more time on them and that we find joy in doing so. That is good. And it is also good to know that we can do all the Lord asks even when we are busy or just starting out.

Daily Activities

Pray twice a day	5 minutes
Read a page or two of the Word	15 minutes

Take time to reflect on how the day went
   before bed   5 minutes
Do your daily work as an act of service   No extra time

Weekly Activities

Attend church   60 minutes plus travel
Do some slightly deeper reflection on your life 15 to 30 minutes
Serve the needy in some way   As much as you choose
Attend to your duties   No extra time
Make time for healthy recreation   May require extra time for some

This list comes to twenty-five minutes a day, with perhaps an additional two hours a week. There will be weeks when we give a lot more time as bigger issues come up or when we are engaged in serious repentance.

Even knowing that the Lord is not asking for a lot of time from us, we need not feel guilty when we don't have much to give. Our job is to do one or two of these things, start to integrate them into our lives, and then add another and another. As we make the Lord the center of our lives, we will notice the miracle of transformations that He performs in us.

LOVE ONE ANOTHER

> *These things I have spoken to you, that My joy may remain in you, and that your joy may be fulfilled. This is My commandment, that you love one another as I have loved you. (John 15:11, 12)*

> *By this all will know that you are My disciples, if you have love for one another. (John 13:35)*

All the activities put forward in this book are called practices of charity, that is, practices of loving the Lord and the people around us. Instead of thinking of these practices as steps or rules, we could think of them as ways to express love. When we turn to the Lord and shun evils, we allow Him to transform us so that we don't harm other people. And when we serve others from sincere motives, we express love for those people and also for the Lord.

Even the external signs of charity are expressions of love. We show that we value the Lord by setting aside time in our day to talk to Him and learn from Him. From all we have read, we can see that the Lord commands us to attend worship, take

Holy Supper, pray, read the Word, and reflect because these activities help us on the path to spiritual living, which is to love Him and others.

Each of us stands at a moment in time, in the presence of the Lord. Every moment is a new beginning, a new opportunity to turn to Him and to love others in new ways. The choice we make in this moment to embrace more fully the spiritual practices the Lord lays out for us takes us one step further on the path into eternity with Him.

> Every smallest fraction of a moment of our life entails a chain of consequences extending into eternity. Indeed every one is like a new beginning to those that follow, and so every single moment of the life both of our understanding and of our will is a new beginning. (AC 3854:3)

Bibliography

In addition to Scripture and Swedenborg's Writings, I have drawn from the following works for this book.

Acton, Elmo. "Use." *New Church Life* 1944: 255-263.

Appelgren, Göran. "Prayer." *New Church Life* 2011: 282-288.

Bayda, Ezra. *Being Zen: Bringing Meditation to Life*. Boston: Shambala, 2003.

Buss, Erik. *Finding the Path: How to Read the Word for Direction and Support*. Bryn Athyn: General Church of the New Jerusalem, 2010.

———. *Freely Give: Evangelization and the New Church*. Bryn Athyn: General Church of the New Jerusalem Office of Evangelization, 2000.

———, *One Heart: Finding True Happiness in Marriage*. Bryn Athyn: General Church of the New Jerusalem, 2006.

Buss, Jared. "Our Shepherd." A sermon preached in Toronto, Canada. March 2018.

Buss, Peter M. "Answers to Prayer." Personal research notes.

Covey, Stephen, A. Roger Merrill, and Rebecca R. Merrill. *First Things First*. New York: Simon & Schuster, 1994.

Cranch, Harold. "Doctrine of Use: The New Moral Law." *New Church Life* 1968: 56-64.

Gladish, Willis. "Reflection." *New Church Life* 1920: 386-393.

Glenn, Coleman. "Remembering the Sabbath." A sermon and accompanying research; received privately.

Hanh, Thích Nhat. *The Miracle of Mindfulness: An Introduction to the Practice of Meditation*. Boston: Beacon Press, 1975.

———. *Peace Is Every Step: The Path of Mindfulness in Everyday Life*. New York: Bantam Books, 1991.

Hauptman, Olaf. "The Third Commandment." Paper presented to the Council of the Clergy of the General Church. June 2011.

Heinrichs, Daniel. "Reflection." *New Church Life* 1965: 404-414.

Keith, Brian. "Seeing the Lord." *New Church Life* 1990: 244-252, 313-319, 365-369.

Odhner, Grant. "Doing Good." Notes for a course at Bryn Athyn College of the New Church Theological School.

———. "Holy Supper.'" Notes for a course at Bryn Athyn College of the New Church Theological School.

———. "Prayer." Notes.

———. "Principles of External Worship." Notes for a course at Bryn Athyn College of the New Church Theological School.

———. "Reflections on the Theme of Reflection" Notes from a presentation at British Academy Summer School. 2006.

———. "Two Tastes of Heaven: a Parallel Between Two Holy Acts." Paper presented to the Council of the Clergy of the General Church. 1986.

———. "Words of Spirit and of Life." *New Church Life* 1987: 417-18, 468-470, 525-527, 575-577, 1988: 21-22, 56-58.

Odhner, John. "Celestial and Spiritual Worship." Paper presented to the Council of the Clergy of the General Church. 1995.

———. "Spiritual Care." Paper presented to the Council of the Clergy of the General Church. June 2017.

Peterson, Eugene. *Subversive Spirituality* Grand. Rapids, MI: William B. Eerdmans Publishing Company, 1997.

Sandström, Erik. "Why and How to Read the Word." *New Church Life* 1976: 66-68.

Smith, Brian. "Reading the Word: Catalog of Quotes." Private research.

———. "Reading the Word." Unpublished pamphlet.

Printed in Great Britain
by Amazon